PR

...terton, G.K.

ROBERT BROWNING

ROBERT BROWNING

BY

G. K. CHESTERTON

MACMILLAN
London · Melbourne · Toronto

ST MARTIN'S PRESS
New York
1967

*This book is copyright in all countries which
are signatories to the Berne Convention*

—

*First published 1903
Macmillan's Pocket Library 1951
Reprinted 1957, 1961, 1964, 1967*

MACMILLAN AND COMPANY LIMITED
*Little Essex Street London WC 2
also Bombay Calcutta Madras Melbourne*

THE MACMILLAN COMPANY OF CANADA LIMITED
70 Bond Street Toronto 2

ST MARTIN'S PRESS INC
175 Fifth Avenue New York NY 10010

PRINTED IN GREAT BRITAIN

CONTENTS

CHAPTER I
BROWNING IN EARLY LIFE 1

CHAPTER II
EARLY WORKS 34

CHAPTER III
BROWNING AND HIS MARRIAGE 55

CHAPTER IV
BROWNING IN ITALY 81

CHAPTER V
BROWNING IN LATER LIFE 105

CHAPTER VI
BROWNING AS A LITERARY ARTIST 133

CHAPTER VII
"THE RING AND THE BOOK" 160

CHAPTER VIII
THE PHILOSOPHY OF BROWNING 177

INDEX 203

ROBERT BROWNING

CHAPTER I

BROWNING IN EARLY LIFE

On the subject of Browning's work innumerable things have been said and remain to be said; of his life, considered as a narrative of facts, there is little or nothing to say. It was a lucid and public and yet quiet life, which culminated in one great dramatic test of character, and then fell back again into this union of quietude and publicity. And yet, in spite of this, it is a great deal more difficult to speak finally about his life than about his work. His work has the mystery which belongs to the complex; his life the much greater mystery which belongs to the simple. He was clever enough to understand his own poetry; and if he understood it, we can understand it. But he was also entirely unconscious and impulsive, and he was never clever enough to understand his own character; consequently we may be excused if that part of him which was hidden from him is partly hidden from us. The subtle man is always immeasurably easier to understand than the natural man; for the subtle man keeps a diary of his moods, he practises the art of self-analysis and self-revelation, and can tell us how he came to feel this or to say that. But a man like Browning knows no more about the state of his emotions than about the state of his pulse; they are things greater than he, things growing at will, like forces of Nature. There is an old anecdote, probably apocryphal, which describes how a feminine admirer wrote to Browning asking him for the meaning of one of his darker poems, and received the following reply: "When that poem was written, two people knew what it meant—God and Robert Browning. And now God only knows what it means." This story gives, in all probability, an entirely false impression of Browning's attitude towards his work. He was a keen artist, a keen scholar, he could put his finger on anything, and he had a memory like the British Museum Library. But the story does, in all probability, give a tolerably accurate picture of Browning's attitude towards his own emotions and his psychological type. If a man had asked him what some particular allusion to a Persian hero meant he could in all probability have quoted half the epic; if a man had asked him which third cousin of Charlemagne was alluded to in *Sordello*, he could have given an account of the man and an account of his father and his grandfather. But if a man had asked him what he thought of himself, or what were his emotions an hour before his wedding, he would have replied with perfect sincerity that God alone knew.

This mystery of the unconscious man, far deeper than any mystery of the conscious one, existing as it does in all men, existed peculiarly in Browning, because he was a very ordinary and spontaneous man. The same thing exists to some extent in all history and all affairs. Anything that is deliberate, twisted, created as a trap and a mystery, must be discovered at last; everything that is done naturally remains mysterious. It may be difficult to discover the principles of the Rosicrucians, but it is much easier to discover the principles of the Rosicrucians than the principles of the United States: nor has any secret society kept its aims so quiet as humanity. The way to be inexplicable is to be chaotic, and on the surface this was the quality of Browning's life; there is the same difference between judging of his poetry and judging of his life, that there is between making a map of a labyrinth and making a map of a mist. The discussion of what some particular allusion in *Sordello* means has gone on so far, and may go on still, but it has it in its nature to end. The life of Robert Browning, who combines the greatest brain with the most simple temperament known in our annals, would go on for ever if we did not decide to summarise it in a very brief and simple narrative.

Robert Browning was born in Camberwell on May 7th 1812. His father and grandfather had been clerks in the Bank of England, and his whole family would appear to have belonged to the solid and educated middle class—the class which is interested in letters, but not ambitious in them, the class to which poetry is a luxury, but not a necessity.

This actual quality and character of the Browning family shows some tendency to be obscured by matters more remote. It is the custom of all biographers to seek for the earliest traces of a family in distant ages and even in distant lands; and Browning, as it happens, has given them opportunities which tend to lead away the mind from the main matter in hand. There is a tradition, for example, that men of his name were prominent in the feudal ages; it is based upon little beyond a coincidence of surnames and the fact that Browning used a seal with a coat-of-arms. Thousands of middle-class men use such a seal, merely because it is a curiosity or a legacy, without knowing or caring anything about the condition of their ancestors in the Middle Ages. Then, again, there is a theory that he was of Jewish blood; a view which is perfectly conceivable, and which Browning would have been the last to have thought derogatory, but for which, as a matter of fact, there is exceedingly little evidence. The chief reason assigned by his contemporaries for the belief was the fact that he was, without doubt, specially and profoundly interested in Jewish matters. This suggestion, worthless in any case, would, if anything, tell the other way. For while an Englishman may be enthusiastic about England, or indignant against England, it never occurred to any living Englishman to be interested in England. Browning was, like every other intelligent Aryan, interested in the Jews; but if he was related to every people in which he was interested, he must have been of extraordinarily mixed extraction. Thirdly, there is the yet more sensational theory that there was in Robert Browning a strain of the negro. The supporters of this hypothesis seem to have little in reality to say, except that Browning's grandmother was certainly a Creole. It is said in support of the view that Browning was singularly dark in early life, and was often mistaken for an Italian. There does not, however, seem to be anything particular to be deduced from this, except that if he looked like an Italian, he must have looked exceedingly unlike a negro.

There is nothing valid against any of these three theories, just as there is nothing valid in their favour; they may, any or all of them, be true, but they are still irrelevant. They are something that is in history or biography a great deal worse than being false—they are misleading. We do not want to know about a man like Browning, whether he had a right to a shield used in the Wars of the Roses, or whether the tenth grandfather of his Creole grandmother had been white or black: we want to know something about his family, which is quite a different thing. We wish to have about Browning not so much the kind of information which would satisfy Clarencieux King-at-Arms, but the sort of information which would satisfy us, if we were advertising for a very confidential secretary, or a very private tutor. We should not be concerned as to whether the tutor were descended from an Irish king, but we should still be really concerned about his extraction, about what manner of people his had been for the last two or three generations. This is the most practical duty of biography, and this is also the most difficult. It is a great deal easier to hunt a family from tombstone to tombstone back to the time of Henry II. than to catch and realise and put upon paper that most nameless and elusive of all things—social tone.

It will be said immediately, and must as promptly be admitted, that we could find a biographical significance in any of these theories if we looked for it. But it is, indeed, the sin and snare of biographers that they tend to see significance in everything; characteristic carelessness if their hero drops his pipe, and characteristic carefulness if he picks it up again. It is true, assuredly, that all the three races above named could be connected with Browning's personality. If we believed, for instance, that he really came of a race of mediæval barons, we should say at once that from them he got his pre-eminent spirit of battle: we should be right, for every line in his stubborn soul and his erect body did really express the fighter; he was always contending, whether it was with a German theory about the Gnostics, or with a stranger who elbowed his wife in a crowd. Again, if we had decided that he was a Jew, we should point out how absorbed he was in the terrible simplicity of monotheism: we should be right, for he was so absorbed. Or again, in the case even of the negro fancy; it would not be difficult for us to suggest a love of colour, a certain mental gaudiness, a pleasure

"When reds and blues were indeed red and blue,"

as he says in *The Ring and the Book*. We should be right; for there really was in Browning a tropical violence of taste, an artistic scheme compounded, as it were, of orchids and cockatoos, which, amid our cold English poets, seems scarcely European. All this is extremely fascinating; and it may be true. But, as has above been suggested, here comes in the great temptation of this kind of work, the noble temptation to see too much in everything. The biographer can easily see a personal significance in these three hypothetical nationalities. But is there in the world a biographer who could lay his hand upon his heart and say that he would not have seen as much significance in any three other nationalities? If Browning's ancestors had been Frenchmen, should we not have said that it was from them doubtless that he inherited that logical agility which marks him among English poets? If his grandfather had been a Swede, should we not have said that the old sea-roving blood broke out in bold speculation and insatiable travel? If his great-aunt had been a Red Indian, should we not have said that only in the Ojibways and the Blackfeet do we find the Browning fantasticality combined with the Browning stoicism? This over-readiness to seize hints is an inevitable part of that secret hero-worship which is the heart of biography. The lover of great men sees signs of them long before they begin to appear on the earth, and, like some old mythological chronicler, claims as their heralds the storms and the falling stars.

A certain indulgence must therefore be extended to the present writer if he declines to follow that admirable veteran of Browning study, Dr. Furnivall, into the prodigious investigations which he has been conducting into the condition of the Browning family since the beginning of the world. For his last discovery, the descent of Browning from a footman in the service of a country magnate, there seems to be suggestive, though not decisive evidence. But Browning's descent from barons, or Jews, or lackeys, or black men, is not the main point touching his family. If the Brownings were of mixed origin, they were so much the more like the great majority of English middle-class people. It is curious that the romance of race should be spoken of as if it were a thing peculiarly aristocratic; that admiration for rank, or interest in family, should mean only interest in one not very interesting type of rank and family. The truth is that aristocrats exhibit less of the romance of pedigree than any other people in the world. For since it is their principle to marry only within their own class and mode of life, there is no opportunity in their case for any of the more interesting studies in heredity; they exhibit almost the unbroken uniformity of the lower animals. It is in the middle classes that we find the poetry of genealogy; it is the suburban grocer standing at his shop door whom some wild dash of Eastern or Celtic blood may drive suddenly to a whole holiday or a crime. Let us admit then, that it is true that these legends of the Browning family have every abstract possibility. But it is a far more cogent and apposite truth that if a man had knocked at the door of every house in the street where Browning was born, he would have found similar legends in all of them. There is hardly a family in Camberwell that has not a story or two about foreign marriages a few generations back; and in all this the Brownings are simply a typical Camberwell family. The real truth about Browning and men like him can scarcely be better expressed than in the words of that very wise and witty story, Kingsley's *Water Babies*, in which the pedigree of the Professor is treated in a manner which is an excellent example of the wild common sense of the book. "His mother was a Dutch woman, and therefore she was born at Curaçao (of course, you have read your geography and therefore know why), and his father was a Pole, and therefore he was brought up at Petropaulowski (of course, you have learnt your modern politics, and therefore know why), but for all that he was as thorough an Englishman as ever coveted his neighbour's goods."

It may be well therefore to abandon the task of obtaining a clear account of Browning's family, and endeavour to obtain, what is much more important, a clear account of his home. For the great central and solid fact, which these heraldic speculations tend inevitably to veil and confuse, is that Browning was a thoroughly typical Englishman of the middle class. He may have had alien blood, and that alien blood, by the paradox we have observed, may have made him more characteristically a native. A phase, a fancy, a metaphor may or may not have been born of eastern or southern elements, but he was, without any question at all, an Englishman of the middle class. Neither all his liberality nor all his learning ever made him anything but an Englishman of the middle class. He expanded his intellectual tolerance until it included the anarchism of *Fifine at the Fair* and the blasphemous theology of Caliban; but he remained himself an Englishman of the middle class. He pictured all the passions of the earth since the Fall, from the devouring amorousness of *Time's Revenges* to the despotic fantasy of *Instans Tyrannus*; but he remained himself an Englishman of the middle class. The moment that he came in contact with anything that was slovenly, anything that was lawless, in actual life, something rose up in him, older than any opinions, the blood of generations of good men. He met George Sand and her poetical circle and hated it, with all the hatred of an old city merchant for the irresponsible life. He met the Spiritualists and hated them, with all the hatred of the middle class for borderlands and equivocal positions and playing with fire. His intellect went upon bewildering voyages, but his soul walked in a straight road. He piled up the fantastic towers of his imagination until they eclipsed the planets; but the plan of the foundation on which he built was always the plan of an honest English house in Camberwell. He abandoned, with a ceaseless intellectual ambition, every one of the convictions of his class; but he carried its prejudices into eternity.

It is then of Browning as a member of the middle class, that we can speak with the greatest historical certainty; and it is his immediate forebears who present the real interest to us. His father, Robert Browning, was a man of great delicacy of taste, and to all appearance of an almost exaggerated delicacy of conscience. Every glimpse we have of him suggests that earnest and almost worried kindliness which is the mark of those to whom selfishness, even justifiable selfishness, is really a thing difficult or impossible. In early life Robert Browning senior was placed by his father (who was apparently a father of a somewhat primitive, not to say barbaric, type) in an important commercial position in the West Indies. He threw up the position however, because it involved him in some recognition of slavery. Whereupon his unique parent, in a transport of rage, not only disinherited him and flung him out of doors, but by a superb stroke of humour, which stands alone in the records of parental ingenuity, sent him in a bill for the cost of his education. About the same time that he was suffering for his moral sensibility he was also disturbed about religious matters, and he completed his severance from his father by joining a dissenting sect. He was, in short, a very typical example of the serious middle-class man of the Wilberforce period, a man to whom duty was all in all, and who would revolutionise an empire or a continent for the satisfaction of a single moral scruple. Thus, while he was Puritan at the core, not the ruthless Puritan of the seventeenth, but the humanitarian Puritan of the eighteenth century, he had upon the surface all the tastes and graces of a man of culture. Numerous accomplishments of the lighter kind, such as drawing and painting in water colours, he possessed; and his feeling for many kinds of literature was fastidious and exact. But the whole was absolutely redolent of the polite severity of the eighteenth century. He lamented his son's early admiration for Byron, and never ceased adjuring him to model himself upon Pope.

He was, in short, one of the old-fashioned humanitarians of the eighteenth century, a class which we may or may not have conquered in moral theory, but which we most certainly have not conquered in moral practice. Robert Browning senior destroyed all his fortunes in order to protest against black slavery; white slavery may be, as later economists tell us, a thing infinitely worse, but not many men destroy their fortunes in order to protest against it. The ideals of the men of that period appear to us very unattractive; to them duty was a kind of chilly sentiment. But when we think what they did with those cold ideals, we can scarcely feel so superior. They uprooted the enormous Upas of slavery, the tree that was literally as old as the race of man. They altered the whole face of Europe with their deductive fancies. We have ideals that are really better, ideals of passion, of mysticism, of a sense of the youth and adventurousness of the earth; but it will be well for us if we achieve as much by our frenzy as they did by their delicacies. It scarcely seems as if we were as robust in our very robustness as they were robust in their sensibility.

Robert Browning's mother was the daughter of

William Wiedermann, a German merchant settled in Dundee, and married to a Scotch wife. One of the poet's principal biographers has suggested that from this union of the German and Scotch, Browning got his metaphysical tendency; it is possible; but here again we must beware of the great biographical danger of making mountains out of molehills. What Browning's mother unquestionably did give to him, was in the way of training—a very strong religious habit, and a great belief in manners. Thomas Carlyle called her "the type of a Scottish gentlewoman," and the phrase has a very real significance to those who realise the peculiar condition of Scotland, one of the very few European countries where large sections of the aristocracy are Puritans; thus a Scottish gentlewoman combines two descriptions of dignity at the same time. Little more is known of this lady except the fact that after her death Browning could not bear to look at places where she had walked.

Browning's education in the formal sense reduces itself to a minimum. In very early boyhood he attended a species of dame-school, which, according to some of his biographers, he had apparently to leave because he was too clever to be tolerable. However this may be, he undoubtedly went afterwards to a school kept by Mr. Ready, at which again he was marked chiefly by precocity. But the boy's education did not in truth take place at any systematic seat of education; it took place in his own home, where one of the quaintest and most learned and most absurdly indulgent of fathers poured out in an endless stream fantastic recitals from the Greek epics and mediæval chronicles. If we test the matter by the test of actual schools and universities, Browning will appear to be almost the least educated man in English literary history. But if we test it by the amount actually learned, we shall think that he was perhaps the most educated man that ever lived; that he was in fact, if anything, over-educated. In a spirited poem he has himself described how, when he was a small child, his father used to pile up chairs in the drawing-room and call them the city of Troy. Browning came out of the home crammed with all kinds of knowledge—knowledge about the Greek poets, knowledge about the Provençal Troubadours, knowledge about the Jewish Rabbis of the Middle Ages. But along with all this knowledge he carried one definite and important piece of ignorance, an ignorance of the degree to which such knowledge was exceptional. He was no spoilt and self-conscious child, taught to regard himself as clever. In the atmosphere in which he lived learning was a pleasure, and a natural pleasure, like sport or wine. He had in it the pleasure of some old scholar of the Renascence, when grammar itself was as fresh as the flowers of spring. He had no reason to suppose that every one did not join in so admirable a game. His sagacious destiny, while giving him knowledge of everything else, left him in ignorance of the ignorance of the world.

Of his boyish days scarcely any important trace remains, except a kind of diary which contains under one date the laconic statement, "Married two wives this morning." The insane ingenuity of the biographer would be quite capable of seeing in this a most suggestive foreshadowing of the sexual dualism which is so ably defended in *Fifine at the Fair*. A great part of his childhood was passed in the society of his only sister Sariana; and it is a curious and touching fact that with her also he passed his last days. From his earliest babyhood he seems to have lived in a more or less stimulating mental atmosphere; but as he emerged into youth he came under great poetic influences, which made his father's classical poetic tradition look for the time insipid. Browning began to live in the life of his own age.

As a young man he attended classes at University College; beyond this there is little evidence that he was much in touch with intellectual circles outside that of his own family. But the forces that were moving the literary world had long passed beyond the merely literary area. About the time of Browning's boyhood a very subtle and profound change was beginning in the intellectual atmosphere of such homes as that of the Brownings. In studying the careers of great men we tend constantly to forget that their youth was generally passed and their characters practically formed in a period long previous to their appearance in history. We think of Milton, the Restoration Puritan, and forget that he grew up in the living shadow of Shakespeare and the full summer of the Elizabethan drama. We realise Garibaldi as a sudden and almost miraculous figure rising about fifty years ago to create the new Kingdom of Italy, and we forget that he must have formed his first ideas of liberty while hearing at his father's dinner-table that Napoleon was the master of Europe. Similarly, we think of Browning as the great Victorian poet, who lived long enough to have opinions on Mr. Gladstone's Home Rule Bill, and forget that as a young man he passed a bookstall and saw a volume ticketed "Mr. Shelley's Atheistic Poem," and had to search even in his own really cultivated circle for some one who could tell him who Mr. Shelley was. Browning was, in short, born in the afterglow of the great Revolution.

The French Revolution was at root a thoroughly optimistic thing. It may seem strange to attribute optimism to anything so destructive; but, in truth, this particular kind of optimism is inevitably, and by its nature, destructive. The great dominant idea of the whole of that period, the period before, during, and long after the Revolution, is the idea that man would by his nature live in an Eden of dignity, liberty and love, and that artificial and decrepit systems are keeping him out of that Eden. No one can do the least justice to the great Jacobins who does not realise that to them breaking the civilisation of ages was like breaking the cords of a treasure-chest. And just as for more than a century great men had dreamed of this beautiful emancipation, so the dream began in the time of Keats and Shelley to creep down among the dullest professions and the most prosaic classes of society. A spirit of revolt was growing among the young of the middle classes, which had nothing at all in common with the complete and pessimistic revolt against all things in heaven or earth, which has been fashionable among the young in more recent times. The Shelleyan enthusiast was altogether on the side of existence; he thought that every cloud and clump of grass shared his strict republican orthodoxy. He represented, in short, a revolt of the normal against the abnormal; he found himself, so to speak, in the heart of a wholly topsy-turvy and blasphemous state of things, in which God was rebelling against Satan. There began to arise about this time a race of young men like Keats, members of a not highly cultivated middle class, and even of classes lower, who felt in a hundred ways this obscure alliance with eternal things against temporal and practical ones, and who lived on its imaginative delight. They were a kind of furtive universalist; they had discovered the whole cosmos, and they kept the whole cosmos a secret. They climbed up dark stairs to meagre garrets, and shut themselves in with the gods. Numbers of the great men, who afterwards illuminated the Victorian era, were at this time living in mean streets in magnificent daydreams. Ruskin was solemnly visiting his solemn suburban aunts; Dickens was going to and fro in a blacking factory; Carlyle, slightly older, was still lingering on a poor farm in Dumfriesshire; Keats had not long become the assistant of the country surgeon when Browning was a boy in Camberwell. On all sides there was the first beginning of the æsthetic stir in the middle classes which expressed itself in the combination of so many poetic lives with so many prosaic livelihoods. It was the age of inspired office-boys.

Browning grew up, then, with the growing fame of Shelley and Keats, in the atmosphere of literary youth, fierce and beautiful, among new poets who believed in a new world. It is important to remember this, because the real Browning was a quite different person from the grim moralist and metaphysician who is seen through the spectacles of Browning Societies and University Extension Lecturers. Browning was first and foremost a poet, a man made to enjoy all things visible and invisible, a priest of the higher passions. The misunderstanding that has supposed him to be other than poetical, because his form was often fanciful and abrupt, is really different from the misunderstanding which attaches to most other poets. The opponents of Victor Hugo called him a mere windbag; the opponents of Shakespeare called him a buffoon. But the admirers of Hugo and Shakespeare at least knew better. Now the admirers and opponents of Browning alike make him out to be a pedant rather than a poet. The only difference between the Browningite and the anti-Browningite, is that the second says he was not a poet but a mere philosopher, and the first says he was a philosopher and not a mere poet. The admirer disparages poetry in order to exalt Browning; the opponent exalts poetry in order to disparage Browning; and all the time Browning himself exalted poetry above all earthly things, served it with single-hearted intensity, and stands among the few poets who hardly wrote a line of anything else.

The whole of the boyhood and youth of Robert Browning has as much the quality of pure poetry as the boyhood and youth of Shelley. We do not find in it any trace of the analytical Browning who is believed in by learned ladies and gentlemen. How indeed would such sympathisers feel if informed that the first poems that Browning wrote in a volume called *Incondita* were noticed to contain the fault of "too much splendour of language and too little wealth of thought"? They were indeed Byronic in the extreme, and Browning in his earlier appearances in society presents himself in quite a romantic manner. Macready, the actor, wrote of him: "He looks and speaks more like a young poet than any one I have ever seen." A picturesque tradition remains that Thomas Carlyle, riding out upon one of his solitary gallops necessitated by his physical sufferings, was stopped by one whom he described as a strangely beautiful youth, who poured out to him without preface or apology his admiration for the great philosopher's works. Browning at this time seems to have left upon many people this impression of physical charm. A friend who attended University College with him says: "He was then a bright handsome youth with long black hair falling over his shoulders." Every tale that remains of him in connection with this period asserts and reasserts the completely romantic spirit by which he was then possessed. He was fond, for example, of following in the track of gipsy caravans, far across country, and a song which he heard with the refrain, "Following the Queen of the Gipsies oh!" rang in his ears long enough to express itself in his soberer and later days in that splendid poem of the spirit of escape and Bohemianism, *The Flight of the Duchess*. Such other of these early glimpses of him as remain, depict him as striding across Wimbledon Common with his hair blowing in the wind, reciting aloud passages from Isaiah, or climbing up into the elms above Norwood to look over London by night. It was when looking down from that suburban eyrie over the whole confounding labyrinth of London that he was filled with that great irresponsible benevolence which is the best of the joys of youth, and conceived the idea of a perfectly irresponsible benevolence in the first plan of *Pippa Passes*. At the end of his father's garden was a laburnum "heavy with its weight of gold," and in the tree two nightingales were in the habit of singing against each other, a form of competition which, I imagine, has since become less common in Camberwell. When Browning as a boy was intoxicated with the poetry of Shelley and Keats, he hypnotised himself into something approaching to a positive conviction that these two birds were the spirits of the two great poets who had settled in a Camberwell garden, in order to sing to the only young gentleman who really adored and understood them. This last story is perhaps the most typical of the tone common to all the rest; it would be difficult to find a story which across the gulf of nearly eighty years awakens so vividly a sense of the sumptuous folly of an intellectual boyhood. With Browning, as with all true poets, passion came first and made intellectual expression, the hunger for beauty making literature as the hunger for bread made a plough. The life he lived in those early days was no life of dull application; there was no poet whose youth was so young. When he was full of years and fame, and delineating in great epics the beauty and horror of the romance of southern Europe, a young man, thinking to please him, said, "There is no romance now except in Italy." "Ah, well," said Browning, "I should like to include poor old Camberwell."

Such glimpses will serve to indicate the kind of essential issue that there was in the nature of things between the generation of Browning and the generation of his father. Browning was bound in the nature of things to become at the outset Byronic, and Byronism was not, of course, in reality so much a pessimism about civilised things as an optimism about savage things. This great revolt on behalf of the elemental which Keats and Shelley represented was bound first of all to occur. Robert Browning junior had to be a part of it, and Robert Browning senior had to go back to his water colours and the faultless couplets of Pope with the full sense of the greatest pathos that the world contains, the pathos of the man who has produced something that he cannot understand.

The earliest works of Browning bear witness, without exception, to this ardent and somewhat sentimental evolution. *Pauline* appeared anonymously in 1833. It exhibits the characteristic mark of a juvenile poem, the general suggestion that the author is a thousand years old. Browning calls it a fragment of a confession; and Mr. Johnson Fox, an old friend of Browning's father, who reviewed it for *Tait's Magazine*, said, with truth, that it would be difficult to find anything more purely confessional. It is the typical confession of a boy laying bare all the spiritual crimes of infidelity and moral waste, in a state of genuine ignorance of the fact that every one else has committed them. It is wholesome and natural for youth to go about confessing that the grass is green, and whispering to a priest hoarsely that it has found a sun in heaven. But the records of that particular period of development, even when they are as ornate and beautiful as *Pauline*, are not necessarily or invariably wholesome reading. The chief interest of *Pauline*, with all its beauties, lies in a certain almost humorous singularity, the fact that Browning, of all people, should have signalised his entrance into the world of letters with a poem which may fairly be called morbid. But this is a morbidity so general and recurrent that it may be called in a contradictory phrase a healthy morbidity; it is a kind of intellectual measles. No one of any degree of maturity in reading *Pauline* will be quite so horrified at the sins of the young gentleman who tells the story as he seems to be himself. It is the utterance of that bitter and heartrending period of youth which comes before we realise the one grand and logical basis of all optimism—the doctrine of original sin. The boy at this stage being an ignorant and inhuman idealist, regards all his faults as frightful secret malformations, and it is only later that he becomes conscious of that large and beautiful and benignant explanation that the heart of man is deceitful above all things and desperately wicked. That Browning, whose judgment on his own work was one of the best in the world, took this view of *Pauline* in after years is quite obvious. He displayed a very manly and unique capacity of really laughing at his own work without being in the least ashamed of it. He said of *Pauline*, "Only this crab remains of the shapely tree of life in my fool's paradise." It would be difficult to express the matter more perfectly. Although *Pauline* was published anonymously, its authorship was known to a certain circle, and Browning began to form friendships in the literary world. He had already become acquainted with two of the best friends he was ever destined to have, Alfred Domett, celebrated in "The Guardian Angel" and "Waring," and his cousin Silverthorne, whose death is spoken of in one of the most perfect lyrics in the English language, Browning's "May and Death." These were men of his own age, and his manner of speaking of them gives us many glimpses into that splendid world of comradeship which Plato and Walt Whitman knew, with its endless days and its immortal nights. Browning had a third friend destined to play an even greater part in his life, but who belonged to an older generation and a statelier school of manners and scholarship. Mr. Kenyon was a schoolfellow of Browning's father, and occupied towards his son something of the position of an irresponsible uncle. He was a rotund, rosy old gentleman, fond of comfort and the courtesies of life, but fond of them more for others, though much for himself. Elizabeth Barrett in after years wrote of "the brightness of his carved speech," which would appear to suggest that he practised that urbane and precise order of wit which was even then old-fashioned. Yet, notwithstanding many talents of this kind, he was not so much an able man as the natural friend and equal of able men.

Browning's circle of friends, however, widened about this time in all directions. One friend in particular he made, the Comte de Ripert-Monclar, a French Royalist with whom he prosecuted with renewed energy his studies in the mediæval and Renaissance schools of philosophy. It was the Count who suggested that Browning should write a poetical play on the subject of Paracelsus. After reflection, indeed, the Count retracted this advice on the ground that the history of the great mystic gave no room for love. Undismayed by this terrible deficiency, Browning caught up the idea with characteristic enthusiasm, and in 1835 appeared the first of his works which he himself regarded as representative—*Paracelsus*. The poem shows an enormous advance in technical literary power; but in the history of Browning's mind it is chiefly interesting as giving an example of a peculiarity which clung to him during the whole of his literary life, an intense love of the holes and corners of history. Fifty-two years afterwards he wrote *Parleyings with certain Persons of Importance in their Day*, the last poem published in his lifetime; and any reader of that remarkable work will perceive that the common characteristic of all these persons is not so much that they were of importance in their day as that they are of no importance in ours. The same eccentric fastidiousness worked in him as a young man when he wrote *Paracelsus* and *Sordello*. Nowhere in Browning's poetry can we find any very exhaustive study of any of the great men who are the favourites of the poet and moralist. He has written about philosophy and ambition and music and morals, but he has written nothing about Socrates or Cæsar or Napoleon, or Beethoven or Mozart, or Buddha or Mahomet. When he wishes to describe a political ambition he selects that entirely unknown individual, King Victor of Sardinia. When he wishes to express the most perfect soul of music, he unearths some extraordinary persons called Abt Vogler and Master Hugues of Saxe-Gotha. When he wishes to express the largest and sublimest scheme of morals and religion which his imagination can conceive, he does not put it into the mouth of any of the great spiritual leaders of mankind, but into the mouth of an obscure Jewish Rabbi of the name of Ben Ezra. It is fully in accordance with this fascinating craze of his that when he wishes to study the deification of the intellect and the disinterested pursuit of the things of the mind, he does not select any of the great philosophers from Plato to Darwin, whose investigations are still of some importance in the eyes of the world. He selects the figure of all figures most covered with modern satire and pity, the *à priori* scientist of the Middle Ages and the Renaissance. His supreme type of the human intellect is neither the academic nor the positivist, but the alchemist. It is difficult to imagine a turn of mind constituting a more complete challenge to the ordinary modern point of view. To the intellect of our time the wild investigators of the school of Paracelsus seem to be the very crown and flower of futility, they are collectors of straws and careful misers of dust. But for all that Browning was right. Any critic who understands the true spirit of mediæval science can see that he was right; no critic can see how right he was unless he understands the spirit of mediæval science as thoroughly as he did. In the character of Paracelsus, Browning wished to paint the dangers and disappointments which attend the man who believes merely in the intellect. He wished to depict the fall of the logician; and with a perfect and unerring instinct he selected a man who wrote and spoke in the tradition of the Middle Ages, the most thoroughly and even painfully logical period that the world has ever seen. If he had chosen an ancient Greek philosopher, it would have been open to the critic to have said that that philosopher relied to some extent upon the most sunny and graceful social life that ever flourished. If he had made him a modern sociological professor, it would have been possible to object that his energies were not wholly concerned with truth, but partly with the solid and material satisfaction of society. But the man truly devoted to the things of the mind was the mediæval magician. It is a remarkable fact that one civilisation does not satisfy itself by calling another civilisation wicked—it calls it uncivilised. We call the Chinese barbarians, and they call us barbarians. The mediæval state, like China, was a foreign civilisation, and this was its supreme characteristic, that it cared for the things of the mind for their own sake. To complain of the researches of its sages on the ground that they were not materially fruitful, is to act as we should act in telling a gardener that his roses were not as digestible as our cabbages. It is not only true that the mediæval philosophers never discovered the steam-engine; it is quite equally true that they never tried. The Eden of the Middle Ages was really a garden, where each of God's flowers—truth and beauty and reason—flourished for its own sake, and with its own name. The Eden of modern progress is a kitchen garden.

It would have been hard, therefore, for Browning to have chosen a better example for his study of intellectual egotism than Paracelsus. Modern life accuses the mediæval tradition of crushing the intellect; Browning, with a truer instinct, accuses that tradition of over-glorifying it. There is, however, another and even more important deduction to be made from the moral of *Paracelsus*. The usual accusation against Browning is that he was consumed with logic; that he thought all subjects to be the proper pabulum of intellectual disquisition; that he gloried chiefly in his own power of plucking knots to pieces and rending fallacies in two; and that to this method he sacrificed deliberately, and with complete self-complacency, the element of poetry and sentiment. To people who imagine Browning to have been this frigid believer in the intellect there is only one answer necessary or sufficient. It is the fact that he wrote a play designed to destroy the whole of this intellectualist fallacy at the age of twenty-three.

Paracelsus was in all likelihood Browning's introduction to the literary world. It was many years, and even many decades, before he had anything like a public appreciation, but a very great part of the minority of those who were destined to appreciate him came over to his standard upon the publication of *Paracelsus*. The celebrated John Forster had taken up *Paracelsus* "as a thing to slate," and had ended its perusal with the wildest curiosity about the author and his works. John Stuart Mill, never backward in generosity, had already interested himself in Browning, and was finally converted by the same poem. Among other early admirers were Landor, Leigh Hunt, Horne, Serjeant Talfourd, and Monckton-Milnes. One man of even greater literary stature seems to have come into Browning's life about this time, a man for whom he never ceased to have the warmest affection and trust. Browning was, indeed, one of the very few men of that period who got on perfectly with Thomas Carlyle. It is precisely one of those little things which speak volumes for the honesty and unfathomable good humour of Browning, that Carlyle, who had a reckless contempt for most other poets of his day, had something amounting to a real attachment to him. He would run over to Paris for the mere privilege of dining with him. Browning, on the other hand, with characteristic impetuosity, passionately defended and justified Carlyle in all companies. "I have just seen dear Carlyle," he writes on one occasion; "catch me calling people dear in a hurry, except in a letter beginning." He sided with Carlyle in the vexed question of the Carlyle domestic relations, and his impression of Mrs. Carlyle was that she was "a hard unlovable woman." As, however, it is on record that he once, while excitedly explaining some point of mystical philosophy, put down Mrs. Carlyle's hot kettle on the hearthrug, any frigidity that he may have observed in her manner may possibly find a natural explanation. His partisanship in the Carlyle affair, which was characteristically headlong and human, may not throw much light on that painful problem itself, but it throws a great deal of light on the character of Browning, which was pugnaciously proud of its friends, and had what may almost be called a lust of loyalty. Browning was not capable of that most sagacious detachment which enabled Tennyson to say that he could not agree that the Carlyles ought never to have married, since if they had each married elsewhere there would have been four miserable people instead of two.

Among the motley and brilliant crowd with which Browning had now begun to mingle, there was no figure more eccentric and spontaneous than that of Macready the actor. This extraordinary person, a man living from hand to mouth in all things spiritual and pecuniary, a man feeding upon flying emotions, conceived something like an attraction towards Browning, spoke of him as the very ideal of a young poet, and in a moment of peculiar excitement suggested to him the writing of a great play. Browning was a man fundamentally indeed more steadfast and prosaic, but on the surface fully as rapid and easily infected as Macready. He immediately began to plan out a great historical play, and selected for his subject "Strafford."

In Browning's treatment of the subject there is something more than a trace of his Puritan and Liberal upbringing. It is one of the very earliest of the really important works in English literature which are based on the Parliamentarian reading of the incidents of the time of Charles I. It is true that the finest element in the play is the opposition between Strafford and Pym, an opposition so complete, so lucid, so consistent, that it has, so to speak, something of the friendly openness and agreement which belongs to an alliance. The two men love each other and fight each other, and do the two things at the same time completely. This is a great thing of which even to attempt the description. It is easy to have the impartiality which can speak judicially of both parties, but it is not so easy to have that larger and higher impartiality which can speak passionately on behalf of both parties. Nevertheless, it may be permissible to repeat that there is in the play a definite trace of Browning's Puritan education and Puritan historical outlook.

For *Strafford* is, of course, an example of that most difficult of all literary works—a political play. The thing has been achieved once at least admirably in Shakespeare's *Julius Cæsar*, and something like it, though from a more one-sided and romantic standpoint, has been done excellently in *L'Aiglon*. But the difficulties of such a play are obvious on the face of the matter. In a political play the principal characters are not merely men. They are symbols, arithmetical figures representing millions of other men outside. It is, by dint of elaborate stage management, possible to bring a mob upon the boards, but the largest mob ever known is nothing but a floating atom of the people; and the people of which the politician has to think does not consist of knots of rioters in the street, but of some million absolutely distinct individuals, each sitting in his own breakfast room reading his own morning paper. To give even the faintest suggestion of the strength and size of the people in this sense in the course of a dramatic performance is obviously impossible. That is why it is so easy on the stage to concentrate all the pathos and dignity upon such persons as Charles I. and Mary Queen of Scots, the vampires of their people, because within the minute limits of a stage there is room for their small virtues and no room for their enormous crimes. It would be impossible to find a stronger example than the case of *Strafford*. It is clear that no one could possibly tell the whole truth about the life and death of Strafford, politically considered, in a play. Strafford was one of the greatest men ever born in England, and he attempted to found a great English official despotism. That is to say, he attempted to found something which is so different from what has actually come about that we can in reality scarcely judge of it, any more than we can judge whether it would be better to live in another planet, or pleasanter to have been born a dog or an elephant. It would require enormous imagination to reconstruct the political ideals of Strafford. Now Browning, as we all know, got over the matter in his play, by practically denying that Strafford had any political ideals at all. That is to say, while crediting Strafford with all his real majesty of intellect and character, he makes the whole of his political action dependent upon his passionate personal attachment to the King. This is unsatisfactory; it is in reality a dodging of the great difficulty of the political play. That difficulty, in the case of any political problem, is, as has been said, great. It would be very hard, for example, to construct a play about Mr. Gladstone's Home Rule Bill. It would be almost impossible to get expressed in a drama of some five acts and some twenty characters anything so ancient and complicated as that Irish problem, the roots of which lie in the darkness of the age of Strongbow, and the branches of which spread out to the remotest commonwealths of the East and West. But we should scarcely be satisfied if a dramatist overcame the difficulty by ascribing Mr. Gladstone's action in the Home Rule question to an overwhelming personal affection for Mr. Healy. And in thus basing Strafford's action upon personal and private reasons, Browning certainly does some injustice to the political greatness of Strafford. To attribute Mr. Gladstone's conversion to Home Rule to an infatuation such as that suggested above, would certainly have the air of implying that the writer thought the Home Rule doctrine a peculiar or untenable one. Similarly, Browning's choice of a motive for Strafford has very much the air of an assumption that there was nothing to be said on public grounds for Strafford's political ideal. Now this is certainly not the case. The Puritans in the great struggles of the reign of Charles I. may have possessed more valuable ideals than the Royalists, but it is a very vulgar error to suppose that they were any more idealistic. In Browning's play Pym is made almost the incarnation of public spirit, and Strafford of private ties. But not only may an upholder of despotism be public-spirited, but in the case of prominent upholders of it like Strafford he generally is. Despotism indeed, and attempts at despotism, like that of Strafford, are a kind of disease of public spirit. They represent, as it were, the drunkenness of responsibility. It is when men begin to grow desperate in their love for the people, when they are overwhelmed with the difficulties and blunders of humanity, that they fall back upon a wild desire to manage everything themselves. Their faith in themselves is only a disillusionment with mankind. They are in that most dreadful position, dreadful alike in personal and public affairs—the position of the man who has lost faith and not lost love. This belief that all would go right if we could only get the strings into our own hands is a fallacy almost without exception, but nobody can justly say that it is not public-spirited. The sin and sorrow of despotism is not that it does not love men, but that it loves them too much and trusts them too little. Therefore from age to age in history arise these great despotic dreamers, whether they be Royalists or Imperialists or even Socialists, who have at root this idea, that the world would enter into rest if it went their way and forswore altogether the right of going its own way. When a man begins to think that the grass will not grow at night unless he lies awake to watch it, he generally ends either in an asylum or on the throne of an Emperor. Of these men Strafford was one, and we cannot but feel that Browning somewhat narrows the significance and tragedy of his place in history by making him merely the champion of a personal idiosyncrasy against a great public demand. Strafford was something greater than this; if indeed, when we come to think of it, a man can be anything greater than the friend of another man. But the whole question is interesting, because Browning, although he never again attacked a political drama of such palpable importance as *Strafford*, could never keep politics altogether out of his dramatic work. *King Victor and King Charles*, which followed it, is a political play, the study of a despotic instinct much meaner than that of Strafford. *Colombe's Birthday*, again, is political as well as romantic. Politics in its historic aspect would seem to have had a great fascination for him, as indeed it must have for all ardent intellects, since it is the one thing in the world that is as intellectual as the *Encyclopædia Britannica* and as rapid as the Derby.

One of the favourite subjects among those who like to conduct long controversies about Browning (and their name is legion) is the question of whether Browning's plays, such as *Strafford*, were successes upon the stage. As they are never agreed about what constitutes a success on the stage, it is difficult to adjudge their quarrels. But the general fact is very simple; such a play as *Strafford* was not a gigantic theatrical success, and nobody, it is to be presumed, ever imagined that it would be. On the other hand, it was certainly not a failure, but was enjoyed and applauded as are hundreds of excellent plays which run only for a week or two, as many excellent plays do, and as all plays ought to do. Above all, the definite success which attended the representation of *Strafford* from the point of view of the more educated and appreciative was quite enough to establish Browning in a certain definite literary position. As a classical and established personality he did not come into his kingdom for years and decades afterwards; not, indeed, until he was near to entering upon the final rest. But as a detached and eccentric personality, as a man who existed and who had arisen on the outskirts of literature, the world began to be conscious of him at this time.

Of what he was personally at the period that he thus became personally apparent, Mrs. Bridell Fox has left a very vivid little sketch. She describes how Browning called at the house (he was acquainted with her father), and finding that gentleman out, asked with a kind of abrupt politeness if he might play on the piano. This touch is very characteristic of the mingled aplomb and unconsciousness of Browning's social manner. "He was then," she writes, "slim and dark, and very handsome, and—may I hint it?—just a trifle of a dandy, addicted to lemon-coloured kid gloves and such things, quite the glass of fashion and the mould of form. But full of 'ambition,' eager for success, eager for fame, and, what is more, determined to conquer fame and to achieve success." That is as good a portrait as we can have of the Browning of these days—a quite self-satisfied, but not self-conscious young man; one who had outgrown, but only just outgrown, the pure romanticism of his boyhood, which made him run after gipsy caravans and listen to nightingales in the wood; a man whose incandescent vitality, now that it had abandoned gipsies and not yet immersed itself in casuistical poems, devoted itself excitedly to trifles, such as lemon-coloured kid gloves and fame. But a man still above all things perfectly young and natural, professing that foppery which follows the fashions, and not that sillier and more demoralising foppery which defies them. Just as he walked in coolly and yet impulsively into a private drawing-room and offered to play, so he walked at this time into the huge and crowded salon of European literature and offered to sing.

CHAPTER II

EARLY WORKS

In 1840 *Sordello* was published. Its reception by the great majority of readers, including some of the ablest men of the time, was a reception of a kind probably unknown in the rest of literary history, a reception that was neither praise nor blame. It was perhaps best expressed by Carlyle, who wrote to say that his wife had read *Sordello* with great interest, and wished to know whether Sordello was a man, or a city, or a book. Better known, of course, is the story of Tennyson, who said that the first line of the poem—

"Who will, may hear Sordello's story told,"

and the last line—

"Who would, has heard Sordello's story told,"

were the only two lines in the poem that he understood, and they were lies.

Perhaps the best story, however, of all the cycle of Sordello legends is that which is related of Douglas Jerrold. He was recovering from an illness; and having obtained permission for the first time to read a little during the day, he picked up a book from a pile beside the bed and began *Sordello*. No sooner had he done so than he turned deadly pale, put down the book, and said, "My God! I'm an idiot. My health is restored, but my mind's gone. I can't understand two consecutive lines of an English poem." He then summoned his family and silently gave the book into their hands, asking for their opinion on the poem; and as the shadow of perplexity gradually passed over their faces, he heaved a sigh of relief and went to sleep. These stories, whether accurate or no, do undoubtedly represent the very peculiar reception accorded to *Sordello*, a reception which, as I have said, bears no resemblance whatever to anything in the way of eulogy or condemnation that had ever been accorded to a work of art before. There had been authors whom it was fashionable to boast of admiring and authors whom it was fashionable to boast of despising; but with *Sordello* enters into literary history the Browning of popular badinage, the author whom it is fashionable to boast of not understanding.

Putting aside for the moment the literary qualities which are to be found in the poem, when it becomes intelligible, there is one question very relevant to the fame and character of Browning which is raised by *Sordello* when it is considered, as most people consider it, as hopelessly unintelligible. It really throws some light upon the reason of Browning's obscurity. The ordinary theory of Browning's obscurity is to the effect that it was a piece of intellectual vanity indulged in more and more insolently as his years and fame increased. There are at least two very decisive objections to this popular explanation. In the first place, it must emphatically be said for Browning that in all the numerous records and impressions of him throughout his long and very public life, there is not one iota of evidence that he was a man who was intellectually vain. The evidence is entirely the other way. He was vain of many things, of his physical health, for example, and even more of the physical health which he contrived to bestow for a certain period upon his wife. From the records of his early dandyism, his flowing hair and his lemon-coloured gloves, it is probable enough that he was vain of his good looks. He was vain of his masculinity, his knowledge of the world, and he was, I fancy, decidedly vain of his prejudices, even, it might be said, vain of being vain of them. But everything is against the idea that he was much in the habit of thinking of himself in his intellectual aspect. In the matter of conversation, for example, some people who liked him found him genial, talkative, anecdotal, with a certain strengthening and sanative quality in his mere bodily presence. Some people who did not like him found him a mere frivolous chatterer, afflicted with bad manners. One lady, who knew him well, said that, though he only met you in a crowd and made some commonplace remark, you went for the rest of the day with your head up. Another lady who did not know him, and therefore disliked him, asked after a dinner party, "Who was that too-exuberant financier?" These are the diversities of feeling about him. But they all agree in one point—that he did not talk cleverly, or try to talk cleverly, as that proceeding is understood in literary circles. He talked positively, he talked a great deal, but he never attempted to give that neat and æsthetic character to his speech which is almost invariable in the case of the man who is vain of his mental superiority. When he did impress people with mental gymnastics, it was mostly in the form of pouring out, with passionate enthusiasm, whole epics written by other people, which is the last thing that the literary egotist would be likely to waste his time over. We have therefore to start with an enormous psychological improbability that Browning made his poems complicated from mere pride in his powers and contempt of his readers.

There is, however, another very practical objection to the ordinary theory that Browning's obscurity was a part of the intoxication of fame and intellectual consideration. We constantly hear the statement that Browning's intellectual complexity increased with his later poems, but the statement is simply not true. *Sordello*, to the indescribable density of which he never afterwards even approached, was begun before *Strafford*, and was therefore the third of his works, and even if we adopt his own habit of ignoring *Pauline*, the second. He wrote the greater part of it when he was twenty-four. It was in his youth, at the time when a man is thinking of love and publicity, of sunshine and singing birds, that he gave birth to this horror of great darkness; and the more we study the matter with any knowledge of the nature of youth, the more we shall come to the conclusion that Browning's obscurity had altogether the opposite origin to that which is usually assigned to it. He was not unintelligible because he was proud, but unintelligible because he was humble. He was not unintelligible because his thoughts were vague, but because to him they were obvious.

A man who is intellectually vain does not make himself incomprehensible, because he is so enormously impressed with the difference between his readers' intelligence and his own that he talks down to them with elaborate repetition and lucidity. What poet was ever vainer than Byron? What poet was ever so magnificently lucid? But a young man of genius who has a genuine humility in his heart does not elaborately explain his discoveries, because he does not think that they are discoveries. He thinks that the whole street is humming with his ideas, and that the postman and the tailor are poets like himself. Browning's impenetrable poetry was the natural expression of this beautiful optimism. *Sordello* was the most glorious compliment that has ever been paid to the average man.

In the same manner, of course, outward obscurity is in a young author a mark of inward clarity. A man who is vague in his ideas does not speak obscurely, because his own dazed and drifting condition leads him to clutch at phrases like ropes and use the formulæ that every one understands. No one ever found Miss Marie Corelli obscure, because she believes only in words. But if a young man really has ideas of his own, he must be obscure at first, because he lives in a world of his own in which there are symbols and correspondences and categories unknown to the rest of the world. Let us take an imaginary example. Suppose that a young poet had developed by himself a peculiar idea that all forms of excitement, including religious excitement, were a kind of evil intoxication, he might say to himself continually that churches were in reality taverns, and this idea would become so fixed in his mind that he would forget that no such association existed in the minds of others. And suppose that in pursuance of this general idea, which is a perfectly clear and intellectual idea, though a very silly one, he were to say that he believed in Puritanism without its theology, and were to repeat this idea also to himself until it became instinctive and familiar, such a man might take up a pen, and under the impression that he was saying something figurative indeed, but quite clear and suggestive, write some such sentence as this, "You will not get the godless Puritan into your white taverns," and no one in the length and breadth of the country could form the remotest notion of what he could mean. So it would have been in any example, for instance, of a man who made some philosophical discovery and did not realise how far the world was from it. If it had been possible for a poet in the sixteenth century to hit upon and learn to regard as obvious the evolutionary theory of Darwin, he might have written down some such line as "the radiant offspring of the ape," and the maddest volumes of mediæval natural history would have been ransacked for the meaning of the allusion. The more fixed and solid and sensible the idea appeared to him, the more dark and fantastic it would have appeared to the world. Most of us indeed, if we ever say anything valuable, say it when we are giving expression to that part of us which has become as familiar and invisible as the pattern on our wall paper. It is only when an idea has become a matter of course to the thinker that it becomes startling to the world.

It is worth while to dwell upon this preliminary point of the ground of Browning's obscurity, because it involves an important issue about him. Our whole view of Browning is bound to be absolutely different, and I think absolutely false, if we start with the conception that he was what the French call an intellectual. If we see Browning with the eyes of his particular followers, we shall inevitably think this. For his followers are pre-eminently intellectuals, and there never lived upon the earth a great man who was so fundamentally different from his followers. Indeed, he felt this heartily and even humorously himself. "Wilkes was no Wilkite," he said, "and I am very far from being a Browningite." We shall, as I say, utterly misunderstand Browning at every step of his career if we suppose that he was the sort of man who would be likely to take a pleasure in asserting the subtlety and abstruseness of his message. He took pleasure beyond all question in himself; in the strictest sense of the word he enjoyed himself. But his conception of himself was never that of the intellectual. He conceived himself rather as a sanguine and strenuous man, a great fighter. "I was ever," as he says, "a fighter." His faults, a certain occasional fierceness and grossness, were the faults that are counted as virtues among navvies and sailors and most primitive men. His virtues, boyishness and absolute fidelity, and a love of plain words and things are the virtues which are counted as vices among the æsthetic prigs who pay him the greatest honour. He had his more objectionable side, like other men, but it had nothing to do with literary egotism. He was not vain of being an extraordinary man. He was only somewhat excessively vain of being an ordinary one.

The Browning then who published *Sordello* we have to conceive, not as a young pedant anxious to exaggerate his superiority to the public, but as a hot-headed, strong-minded, inexperienced, and essentially humble man, who had more ideas than he knew how to disentangle from each other. If we compare, for example, the complexity of Browning with the clarity of Matthew Arnold, we shall realise that the cause lies in the fact that Matthew Arnold was an intellectual aristocrat, and Browning an intellectual democrat. The particular peculiarities of *Sordello* illustrate the matter very significantly. A very great part of the difficulty of *Sordello*, for instance, is in the fact that before the reader even approaches to tackling the difficulties of Browning's actual narrative, he is apparently expected to start with an exhaustive knowledge of that most shadowy and bewildering of all human epochs—the period of the Guelph and Ghibelline struggles in mediæval Italy. Here, of course, Browning simply betrays that impetuous humility which we have previously observed. His father was a student of mediæval chronicles, he had himself imbibed that learning in the same casual manner in which a boy learns to walk or to play cricket. Consequently in a literary sense he rushed up to the first person he met and began talking about Ecelo and Taurello Salinguerra with about as much literary egotism as an English baby shows when it talks English to an Italian organ grinder. Beyond this the poem of *Sordello*, powerful as it is, does not present any very significant advance in Browning's mental development on that already represented by *Pauline* and *Paracelsus*. *Pauline*, *Paracelsus*, and *Sordello* stand together in the general fact that they are all, in the excellent phrase used about the first by Mr. Johnson Fox, "confessional." All three are analyses of the weakness which every artistic temperament finds in itself. Browning is still writing about himself, a subject of which he, like all good and brave men, was profoundly ignorant. This kind of self-analysis is always misleading. For we do not see in ourselves those dominant traits strong enough to force themselves out in action which our neighbours see. We see only a welter of minute mental experiences which include all the sins that were ever committed by Nero or Sir Willoughby Patterne. When studying ourselves, we are looking at a fresco with a magnifying glass. Consequently, these early impressions which great men have given of themselves are nearly always slanders upon themselves, for the strongest man is weak to his own conscience, and Hamlet flourished to a certainty even inside Napoleon. So it was with Browning, who when he was nearly eighty was destined to write with the hilarity of a schoolboy, but who wrote in his boyhood poems devoted to analysing the final break-up of intellect and soul.

Sordello, with all its load of learning, and almost more oppressive load of beauty, has never had any very important influence even upon Browningites, and with the rest of the world the name has passed into a jest. The most truly memorable thing about it was Browning's saying in answer to all gibes and misconceptions, a saying which expresses better than anything else what genuine metal was in him, "I blame no one, least of all myself, who did my best then and since." This is indeed a model for all men of letters who do not wish to retain only the letters and to lose the man.

When next Browning spoke, it was from a greater height and with a new voice. His visit to Asolo, " his first love," as he said, "among Italian cities," coincided with the stir and transformation in his spirit and the breaking up of that splendid palace of mirrors in which a man like Byron had lived and died. In 1841 *Pippa Passes* appeared, and with it the real Browning of the modern world. He had made the discovery which Byron never made, but which almost every young man does at last make—the thrilling discovery that he is not Robinson Crusoe. *Pippa Passes* is the greatest poem ever written, with the exception of one or two by Walt Whitman, to express the sentiment of the pure love of humanity. The phrase has unfortunately a false and pedantic sound. The love of humanity is a thing supposed to be professed only by vulgar and officious philanthropists, or by saints of a superhuman detachment and universality. As a matter of fact, love of humanity is the commonest and most natural of the feelings of a fresh nature, and almost every one has felt it alight capriciously upon him when looking at a crowded park or a room full of dancers. The love of those whom we do not know is quite as eternal a sentiment as the love of those whom we do know. In our friends the richness of life is proved to us by what we have gained; in the faces in the street the richness of life is proved to us by the hint of what we have lost. And this feeling for strange faces and strange lives, when it is felt keenly by a young man, almost always expresses itself in a desire after a kind of vagabond beneficence, a desire to go through the world scattering goodness like a capricious god. It is desired that mankind should hunt in vain for its best friend as it would hunt for a criminal; that he should be an anonymous Saviour, an unrecorded Christ. Browning, like every one else, when awakened to the beauty and variety of men, dreamed of this arrogant self-effacement. He has written of himself that he had long thought vaguely of a being passing through the world, obscure and unnameable, but moulding the destinies of others to mightier and better issues. Then his almost faultless artistic instinct came in and suggested that this being, whom he dramatised as the work-girl, Pippa, should be even unconscious of anything but her own happiness, and should sway men's lives with a lonely mirth. It was a bold and moving conception to show us these mature and tragic human groups all at the supreme moment eavesdropping upon the solitude of a child. And it was an even more precise instinct which made Browning make the errant benefactor a woman. A man's good work is effected by doing what he does, a woman's by being what she is.

There is one other point about *Pippa Passes* which is worth a moment's attention. The great difficulty with regard to the understanding of Browning is the fact that, to all appearance, scarcely any one can be induced to take him seriously as a literary artist. His adversaries consider his literary vagaries a disqualification for every position among poets; and his admirers regard those vagaries with the affectionate indulgence of a circle of maiden aunts towards a boy home for the holidays. Browning is supposed to do as he likes with form, because he had such a profound scheme of thought. But, as a matter of fact, though few of his followers will take Browning's literary form seriously, he took his own literary form very seriously. Now *Pippa Passes* is, among other things, eminently remarkable as a very original artistic form, a series of disconnected but dramatic scenes which have only in common the appearance of one figure. For this admirable literary departure Browning, amid all the laudations of his "mind" and his "message," has scarcely ever had credit. And just as we should, if we took Browning seriously as a poet, see that he had made many noble literary forms, so we should also see that he did make from time to time certain definite literary mistakes. There is one of them, a glaring one, in *Pippa Passes*; and, as far as I know, no critic has ever thought enough of Browning as an artist to point it out. It is a gross falsification of the whole beauty of *Pippa Passes* to make the Monsignor and his brother's accomplice in the last act discuss a plan touching the fate of Pippa herself. The whole central and splendid idea of the drama is the fact that Pippa is utterly remote from the grand folk whose lives she troubles and transforms. To make her in the end turn out to be the niece of one of them, is like a whiff from an Adelphi melodrama, an excellent thing in its place, but destructive of the entire conception of Pippa. Having done that, Browning might just as well have made Sebald turn out to be her long lost brother, and Luigi a husband to whom she was secretly married. Browning made this mistake when his own splendid artistic power was only growing, and its merits and its faults in a tangle. But its real literary merits and its real literary faults have alike remained unrecognised under the influence of that unfortunate intellectualism which idolises Browning as a metaphysician and neglects him as a poet. But a better test was coming. Browning's poetry, in the most strictly poetical sense, reached its flower in *Dramatic Lyrics*, published in 1842. Here he showed himself a picturesque and poignant artist in a wholly original manner. And the two main characteristics of the work were the two characteristics most commonly denied to Browning, both by his opponents and his followers, passion and beauty; but beauty had enlarged her boundaries in new modes of dramatic arrangement, and passion had found new voices in fantastic and realistic verse. Those who suppose Browning to be a wholly philosophic poet, number a great majority of his commentators. But when we come to look at the actual facts, they are strangely and almost unexpectedly otherwise.

Let any one who believes in the arrogantly intellectual character of Browning's poetry run through the actual répertoire of the *Dramatic Lyrics*. The first item consists of those splendid war chants called "Cavalier Tunes." I do not imagine that any one will maintain that there is any very mysterious metaphysical aim in them. The second item is the fine poem "The Lost Leader," a poem which expresses in perfectly lucid and lyrical verse a perfectly normal and old-fashioned indignation. It is the same, however far we carry the query. What theory does the next poem, "How they brought the Good News from Ghent to Aix," express, except the daring speculation that it is often exciting to ride a good horse in Belgium? What theory does the poem after that, "Through the Metidja to Abd-el-Kadr," express, except that it is also frequently exciting to ride a good horse in Africa? Then comes "Nationality in Drinks," a mere technical oddity without a gleam of philosophy; and after that those two entirely exquisite "Garden Fancies," the first of which is devoted to the abstruse thesis that a woman may be charming, and the second to the equally abstruse thesis that a book may be a bore. Then comes "The Soliloquy of the Spanish Cloister," from which the most ingenious "Browning student" cannot extract anything except that people sometimes hate each other in Spain; and then "The Laboratory," from which he could extract nothing except that people sometimes hate each other in France. This is a perfectly honest record of the poems as they stand. And the first eleven poems read straight off are remarkable for these two obvious characteristics—first, that they contain not even a suggestion of anything that could be called philosophy; and second, that they contain a considerable proportion of the best and most typical poems that Browning ever wrote. It may be repeated that either he wrote these lyrics because he had an artistic sense, or it is impossible to hazard even the wildest guess as to why he wrote them.

It is permissible to say that the *Dramatic Lyrics* represent the arrival of the real Browning of literary history. It is true that he had written already many admirable poems of a far more ambitious plan—*Paracelsus* with its splendid version of the faults of the intellectual, *Pippa Passes* with its beautiful deification of unconscious influence. But youth is always ambitious and universal; mature work exhibits more of individuality, more of the special type and colour of work which a man is destined to do. Youth is universal, but not individual. The genius who begins life with a very genuine and sincere doubt whether he is meant to be an exquisite and idolised violinist, or the most powerful and eloquent Prime Minister of modern times, does at last end by making the discovery that there is, after all, one thing, possibly a certain style of illustrating Nursery Rhymes, which he can really do better than any one else. This was what happened to Browning; like every one else, he had to discover first the universe, and then humanity, and at last himself. With him, as with all others, the great paradox and the great definition of life was this, that the ambition narrows as the mind expands. In *Dramatic Lyrics* he discovered the one thing that he could really do better than any one else—the dramatic lyric. The form is absolutely original: he had discovered a new field of poetry, and in the centre of that field he had found himself.

The actual quality, the actual originality of the form is a little difficult to describe. But its general characteristic is the fearless and most dexterous use of grotesque things in order to express sublime emotions. The best and most characteristic of the poems are love-poems; they express almost to perfection the real wonderland of youth, but they do not express it by the ideal imagery of most poets of love. The imagery of these poems consists, if we may take a rapid survey of Browning's love poetry, of suburban streets, straws, garden-rakes, medicine bottles, pianos, window-blinds, burnt cork, fashionable fur coats. But in this new method he thoroughly expressed the true essential, the insatiable realism of passion. If any one wished to prove that Browning was not, as he is said to be, the poet of thought, but pre-eminently one of the poets of passion, we could scarcely find a better evidence of this profoundly passionate element than Browning's astonishing realism in love poetry. There is nothing so fiercely realistic as sentiment and emotion. Thought and the intellect are content to accept abstractions, summaries, and generalisations; they are content that ten acres of ground should be called for the sake of argument X, and ten widows' incomes called for the sake of argument Y; they are content that a thousand awful and mysterious disappearances from the visible universe should be summed up as the mortality of a district, or that ten thousand intoxications of the soul should bear the general name of the instinct of sex. Rationalism can live upon air and signs and numbers. But sentiment must have reality; emotion demands the real fields, the real widows' homes, the real corpse, and the real woman. And therefore Browning's love poetry is the finest love poetry in the world, because it does not talk about raptures and ideals and gates of heaven, but about window-panes and gloves and garden walls. It does not deal much with abstractions; it is the truest of all love poetry, because it does not speak much about love. It awakens in every man the memories of that immortal instant when common and dead things had a meaning beyond the power of any dictionary to utter, and a value beyond the power of any millionaire to compute. He expresses the celestial time when a man does not think about heaven, but about a parasol. And therefore he is, first, the greatest of love poets, and, secondly, the only optimistic philosopher except Whitman.

The general accusation against Browning in connection with his use of the grotesque comes in very definitely here; for in using these homely and practical images, these allusions, bordering on what many would call the commonplace, he was indeed true to the actual and abiding spirit of love. In that delightful poem "Youth and Art" we have the singing girl saying to her old lover—

> "No harm! It was not my fault
> If you never turned your eye's tail up
> As I shook upon E *in alt*,
> Or ran the chromatic scale up."

This is a great deal more like the real chaff that passes between those whose hearts are full of new hope or of old memory than half the great poems of the world. Browning never forgets the little details which to a man who has ever really lived may suddenly send an arrow through the heart. Take, for example, such a matter as dress, as it is treated in "A Lover's Quarrel."

> "See, how she looks now, dressed
> In a sledging cap and vest!
> 'Tis a huge fur cloak—
> Like a reindeer's yoke
> Falls the lappet along the breast:
> Sleeves for her arms to rest,
> Or to hang, as my Love likes best."

That would almost serve as an order to a dressmaker, and is therefore poetry, or at least excellent poetry of this order. So great a power have these dead things of taking hold on the living spirit, that I question whether any one could read through the catalogue of a miscellaneous auction sale without coming upon things which, if realised for a moment, would be near to the elemental tears. And if any of us or all of us are truly optimists, and believe as Browning did, that existence has a value wholly inexpressible, we are most truly compelled to that sentiment not by any argument or triumphant justification of the cosmos, but by a few of these momentary and immortal sights and sounds, a gesture, an old song, a portrait, a piano, an old door.

In 1843 appeared that marvellous drama *The Return of the Druses*, a work which contains more of Browning's typical qualities exhibited in an exquisite literary shape, than can easily be counted. We have in *The Return of the Druses* his love of the corners of history, his interest in the religious mind of the East, with its almost terrifying sense of being in the hand of heaven, his love of colour and verbal luxury, of gold and green and purple, which made some think he must be an Oriental himself. But, above all, it presents the first rise of that great psychological ambition which Browning was thenceforth to pursue. In *Pauline* and the poems that follow it, Browning has only the comparatively easy task of giving an account of himself. In *Pippa Passes* he has the only less easy task of giving an account of humanity. In *The Return of the Druses* he has for the first time the task which is so much harder than giving an account of humanity—the task of giving an account of a human being. Djabal, the great Oriental impostor, who is the central character of the play, is a peculiarly subtle character, a compound of blasphemous and lying assumptions of Godhead with genuine and stirring patriotic and personal feelings: he is a blend, so to speak, of a base divinity and of a noble humanity. He is supremely important in the history of Browning's mind, for he is the first of that great series of the apologiæ of apparently evil men, on which the poet was to pour out so much of his imaginative wealth— Djabal, Fra Lippo, Bishop Blougram, Sludge, Prince Hohenstiel-Schwangau, and the hero of *Fifine at the Fair*.

With this play, so far as any point can be fixed for the matter, he enters for the first time on the most valuable of all his labours—the defence of the indefensible. It may be noticed that Browning was not in the least content with the fact that certain human frailties had always lain more or less under an implied indulgence; that all human sentiment had agreed that a profligate might be generous, or that a drunkard might be high-minded. He was insatiable: he wished to go further and show in a character like Djabal that an impostor might be generous and that a liar might be high-minded. In all his life, it must constantly be remembered, he tried always the most difficult things. Just as he tried the queerest metres and attempted to manage them, so he tried the queerest human souls and attempted to stand in their place. Charity was his basic philosophy; but it was, as it were, a fierce charity, a charity that went man-hunting. He was a kind of cosmic detective who walked into the foulest of thieves' kitchens and accused men publicly of virtue. The character of Djabal in *The Return of the Druses* is the first of this long series of forlorn hopes for the relief of long surrendered castles of misconduct. As we shall see, even realising the humanity of a noble impostor like Djabal did not content his erratic hunger for goodness. He went further again, and realised the humanity of a mean impostor like Sludge. But in all things he retained this essential characteristic, that he was not content with seeking sinners—he sought the sinners whom even sinners cast out.

Browning's feeling of ambition in the matter of the drama continued to grow at this time. It must be remembered that he had every natural tendency to be theatrical, though he lacked the essential lucidity. He was not, as a matter of fact, a particularly unsuccessful dramatist; but in the world of abstract temperaments he was by nature an unsuccessful dramatist. He was, that is to say, a man who loved above all things plain and sensational words, open catastrophes, a clear and ringing conclusion to everything. But it so happened, unfortunately, that his own words were not plain; that his catastrophes came with a crashing and sudden unintelligibleness which left men in doubt whether the thing were a catastrophe or a great stroke of good luck; that his conclusion, though it rang like a trumpet to the four corners of heaven, was in its actual message quite inaudible. We are bound to admit, on the authority of all his best critics and admirers, that his plays were not failures, but we can all feel that they should have been. He was, as it were, by nature a neglected dramatist. He was one of those who achieve the reputation, in the literal sense, of eccentricity by their frantic efforts to reach the centre.

A Blot on the 'Scutcheon followed *The Return of the Druses*. In connection with the performance of this very fine play a quarrel arose which would not be worth mentioning if it did not happen to illustrate the curious energetic simplicity of Browning's character. Macready, who was in desperately low financial circumstances at this time, tried by every means conceivable to avoid playing the part; he dodged, he shuffled, he tried every evasion that occurred to him, but it never occurred to Browning to see what he meant. He pushed off the part upon Phelps, and Browning was contented; he resumed it, and Browning was only discontented on behalf of Phelps. The two had a quarrel; they were both headstrong, passionate men, but the quarrel dealt entirely with the unfortunate condition of Phelps. Browning beat down his own hat over his eyes; Macready flung Browning's manuscript with a slap upon the floor. But all the time it never occurred to the poet that Macready's conduct was dictated by anything so crude and simple as a desire for money. Browning was in fact by his principles and his ideals a man of the world, but in his life far otherwise. That worldly ease which is to most of us a temptation was to him an ideal. He was as it were a citizen of the New Jerusalem who desired with perfect sanity and simplicity to be a citizen of Mayfair. There was in him a quality which can only be most delicately described; for it was a virtue which bears a strange resemblance to one of the meanest of vices. Those curious people who think the truth a thing that can be said violently and with ease, might naturally call Browning a snob. He was fond of society, of fashion and even of wealth: but there is no snobbery in admiring these things or any things if we admire them for the right reasons. He admired them as worldlings cannot admire them: he was, as it were, the child who comes in with the dessert. He bore the same relation to the snob that the righteous man bears to the Pharisee: something frightfully close and similar and yet an everlasting opposite.

CHAPTER III

BROWNING AND HIS MARRIAGE

ROBERT BROWNING had his faults, and the general direction of those faults has been previously suggested. The chief of his faults, a certain uncontrollable brutality of speech and gesture when he was strongly roused, was destined to cling to him all through his life, and to startle with the blaze of a volcano even the last quiet years before his death. But any one who wishes to understand how deep was the elemental honesty and reality of his character, how profoundly worthy he was of any love that was bestowed upon him, need only study one most striking and determining element in the question — Browning's simple, heartfelt, and unlimited admiration for other people. He was one of a generation of great men, of great men who had a certain peculiar type, certain peculiar merits and defects. Carlyle, Tennyson, Ruskin, Matthew Arnold, were alike in being children of a very strenuous and conscientious age, alike in possessing its earnestness and air of deciding great matters, alike also in showing a certain almost noble jealousy, a certain restlessness, a certain fear of other influences. Browning alone had no fear; he welcomed, evidently without the least affectation, all the influences of his day. A very interesting letter of his remains in which he describes his pleasure in a university dinner. "Praise," he says in effect, "was given very deservedly to Matthew Arnold and Swinburne, and to that pride of Oxford men, Clough." The really striking thing about these three names is the fact that they are united in Browning's praise in a way in which they are by no means united in each other's. Matthew Arnold, in one of his extant letters, calls Swinburne "a young pseudo-Shelley," who, according to Arnold, thinks he can make Greek plays good by making them modern. Mr. Swinburne, on the other hand, has summarised Clough in a contemptuous rhyme:—

> "There was a bad poet named Clough,
> Whom his friends all united to puff.
> But the public, though dull,
> Has not quite such a skull
> As belongs to believers in Clough."

The same general fact will be found through the whole of Browning's life and critical attitude. He adored Shelley, and also Carlyle who sneered at him. He delighted in Mill, and also in Ruskin who rebelled against Mill. He excused Napoleon III. and Landor who hurled interminable curses against Napoleon. He admired all the cycle of great men who all contemned each other. To say that he had no streak of envy in his nature would be true, but unfair; for there is no justification for attributing any of these great men's opinions to envy. But Browning was really unique, in that he had a certain spontaneous and unthinking tendency to the admiration of others. He admired another poet as he admired a fading sunset or a chance spring leaf. He no more thought whether he could be as good as that man in that department than whether he could be redder than the sunset or greener than the leaf of spring. He was naturally magnanimous in the literal sense of that sublime word; his mind was so great that it rejoiced in the triumphs of strangers. In this spirit Browning had already cast his eyes round in the literary world of his time, and had been greatly and justifiably struck with the work of a young lady poet, Miss Barrett.

That impression was indeed amply justified. In a time when it was thought necessary for a lady to dilute the wine of poetry to its very weakest tint, Miss Barrett had contrived to produce poetry which was open to literary objection as too heady and too high-coloured. When she erred it was through an Elizabethan audacity and luxuriance, a straining after violent metaphors. With her reappeared in poetry a certain element which had not been present in it since the last days of Elizabethan literature, the fusion of the most elementary human passion with something which can only be described as wit, a certain love of quaint and sustained similes, of parallels wildly logical, and of brazen paradox and antithesis. We find this hot wit, as distinct from the cold wit of the school of Pope, in the puns and buffooneries of Shakespeare. We find it lingering in *Hudibras*, and we do not find it again until we come to such strange and strong lines as these of Elizabeth Barrett in her poem on Napoleon :—

"Blood fell like dew beneath his sunrise—sooth,
But glittered dew-like in the covenanted
And high-rayed light. He was a despot—granted,
But the αὐτός of his autocratic mouth
Said 'Yea' i' the people's French ! He magnified
The image of the freedom he denied."

Her poems are full of quaint things, of such things as the eyes in the peacock fans of the Vatican, which she describes as winking at the Italian tricolor. She often took the step from the sublime to the ridiculous: but to take this step one must reach the sublime. Elizabeth Barrett contrived to assert, what still needs but then urgently needed assertion, the fact that womanliness, whether in life or poetry, was a positive thing, and not the negative of manliness. Her verse at its best was quite as strong as Browning's own, and very nearly as clever. The difference between their natures was a difference between two primary colours, not between dark and light shades of the same colour.

Browning had often heard not only of the public, but of the private life of this lady from his father's friend Kenyon. The old man, who was one of those rare and valuable people who have a talent for establishing definite relationships with people after a comparatively short intercourse, had been appointed by Miss Barrett as her "fairy godfather." He spoke much about her to Browning, and of Browning to her, with a certain courtly garrulity which was one of his talents. And there could be little doubt that the two poets would have met long before had it not been for certain peculiarities in the position of Miss Barrett. She was an invalid, and an invalid of a somewhat unique kind, and living beyond all question under very unique circumstances.

Her father, Edward Moulton Barrett, had been a landowner in the West Indies, and thus, by a somewhat curious coincidence, had borne a part in the same social system which stung Browning's father into revolt and renunciation. The part played by Edward

Barrett, however, though little or nothing is known of it, was probably very different. He was a man Conservative by nature, a believer in authority in the nation and the family, and endowed with some faculties for making his conceptions prevail. He was an able man, capable in his language of a certain bitter felicity of phrase. He was rigidly upright and responsible, and he had a capacity for profound affection. But selfishness of the most perilous sort, an unconscious selfishness, was eating away his moral foundations, as it tends to eat away those of all despots. His most fugitive moods changed and controlled the whole atmosphere of the house, and the state of things was fully as oppressive in the case of his good moods as in the case of his bad ones. He had, what is perhaps the subtlest and worst spirit of egotism, not that spirit merely which thinks that nothing should stand in the way of its ill-temper, but that spirit which thinks that nothing should stand in the way of its amiability. His daughters must be absolutely at his beck and call, whether it was to be brow-beaten or caressed. During the early years of Elizabeth Barrett's life, the family had lived in the country, and for that brief period she had known a more wholesome life than she was destined ever to know again until her marriage long afterwards. She was not, as is the general popular idea, absolutely a congenital invalid, weak, and almost moribund from the cradle. In early girlhood she was slight and sensitive indeed, but perfectly active and courageous. She was a good horsewoman, and the accident which handicapped her for so many years afterwards happened to her when she was riding. The injury to her spine, however, will be found, the more we study her history, to be only one of the influences which were to darken those bedridden years, and to have among them a far less important place than has hitherto been attached to it. Her father moved to a melancholy house in Wimpole Street; and his own character growing gloomier and stranger as time went on, he mounted guard over his daughter's sickbed in a manner compounded of the pessimist and the disciplinarian. She was not permitted to stir from the sofa, often not even to cross two rooms to her bed. Her father came and prayed over her with a kind of melancholy glee, and with the avowed solemnity of a watcher by a deathbed. She was surrounded by that most poisonous and degrading of all atmospheres—a medical atmosphere. The existence of this atmosphere has nothing to do with the actual nature or prolongation of disease. A man may pass three hours out of every five in a state of bad health, and yet regard, as Stevenson regarded, the three hours as exceptional and the two as normal. But the curse that lay on the Barrett household was the curse of considering ill-health the natural condition of a human being. The truth was that Edward Barrett was living emotionally and æsthetically, like some detestable decadent poet, upon his daughter's decline. He did not know this, but it was so. Scenes, explanations, prayers, fury, and forgiveness had become bread and meat for which he hungered; and when the cloud was upon his spirit, he would lash out at all things and every one with the insatiable cruelty of the sentimentalist.

It is wonderful that Elizabeth Barrett was not made

thoroughly morbid and impotent by this intolerable violence and more intolerable tenderness. In her estimate of her own health she did, of course, suffer. It is evident that she practically believed herself to be dying. But she was a high-spirited woman, full of that silent and quite unfathomable kind of courage which is only found in women, and she took a much more cheerful view of death than her father did of life. Silent rooms, low voices, lowered blinds, long days of loneliness, and of the sickliest kind of sympathy, had not tamed a spirit which was swift and headlong to a fault. She could still own with truth the magnificent fact that her chief vice was impatience, "tearing open parcels instead of untying them;" looking at the end of books before she had read them was, she said, incurable with her. It is difficult to imagine anything more genuinely stirring than the achievement of this woman, who thus contrived, while possessing all the excuses of an invalid, to retain some of the faults of a tomboy.

Impetuosity, vividness, a certain absoluteness and urgency in her demands, marked her in the eyes of all who came in contact with her. In after years, when Browning had experimentally shaved his beard off, she told him with emphatic gestures that it must be grown again "that minute." There we have very graphically the spirit which tears open parcels. Not in vain, or as a mere phrase, did her husband after her death describe her as "all a wonder and a wild desire."

She had, of course, lived her second and real life in literature and the things of the mind, and this in a very genuine and strenuous sense. Her mental occupations were not mere mechanical accomplishments almost as colourless as the monotony they relieved, nor were they coloured in any visible manner by the unwholesome atmosphere in which she breathed. She used her brains seriously; she was a good Greek scholar, and had read Æschylus and Euripides unceasingly with her blind friend, Mr. Boyd; and she had, and retained even to the hour of her death, a passionate and quite practical interest in great public questions. Naturally she was not uninterested in Robert Browning, but it does not appear that she felt at this time the same kind of fiery artistic curiosity that he felt about her. He does appear to have felt an attraction, which may almost be called mystical, for the personality which was shrouded from the world by such sombre curtains. In 1845 he addressed a letter to her in which he spoke of a former occasion on which they had nearly met, and compared it to the sensation of having once been outside the chapel of some marvellous illumination and found the door barred against him. In that phrase it is easy to see how much of the romantic boyhood of Browning remained inside the resolute man of the world into which he was to all external appearance solidifying. Miss Barrett replied to his letters with charming sincerity and humour, and with much of that leisurely self-revelation which is possible for an invalid who has nothing else to do. She herself, with her love of quiet and intellectual companionship, would probably have been quite happy for the rest of her life if their relations had always remained a learned and delightful correspondence. But she must have known very little of Robert Browning if she imagined he would be contented with this airy and bloodless tie. At all times of his life he was sufficiently fond of his own way; at this time he was especially prompt and impulsive, and he had always a great love for seeing and hearing and feeling people, a love of the physical presence of friends, which made him slap men on the back and hit them in the chest when he was very fond of them. The correspondence between the two poets had not long begun when Browning suggested something which was almost a blasphemy in the Barrett household, that he should come and call on her as he would on any one else. This seems to have thrown her into a flutter of fear and doubt. She alleges all kinds of obstacles, the chief of which were her health and the season of the year and the east winds. "If my truest heart's wishes avail," replied Browning obstinately, "you shall laugh at east winds yet as I do."

Then began the chief part of that celebrated correspondence which has within comparatively recent years been placed before the world. It is a correspondence which has very peculiar qualities and raises many profound questions.

It is impossible to deal at any length with the picture given in these remarkable letters of the gradual progress and amalgamation of two spirits of great natural potency and independence, without saying at least a word about the moral question raised by their publication and the many expressions of disapproval which it entails. To the mind of the present writer the whole of such a question should be tested by one perfectly clear intellectual distinction and comparison. I am not prepared to admit that there is or can be, properly speaking, in the world anything that is too sacred to be known. That spiritual beauty and spiritual truth are in their nature communicable, and that they should be communicated, is a principle which lies at the root of every conceivable religion. Christ was crucified upon a hill, and not in a cavern, and the word Gospel itself involves the same idea as the ordinary name of a daily paper. Whenever, therefore, a poet or any similar type of man can, or conceives that he can, make all men partakers in some splendid secret of his own heart, I can imagine nothing saner and nothing manlier than his course in doing so. Thus it was that Dante made a new heaven and a new hell out of a girl's nod in the streets of Florence. Thus it was that Paul founded a civilisation by keeping an ethical diary. But the one essential which exists in all such cases as these is that the man in question believes that he can make the story as stately to the whole world as it is to him, and he chooses his words to that end. Yet when a work contains expressions which have one value and significance when read by the people to whom they were addressed, and an entirely different value and significance when read by any one else, then the element of the violation of sanctity does arise. It is not because there is anything in this world too sacred to tell. It is rather because there are a great many things in this world too sacred to parody. If Browning could really convey to the world the inmost core of his affection for his wife, I see no reason why he should not. But the objection to letters which begin "My dear Ba," is that they do not convey anything of the sort. As far as any third person is concerned, Browning might as well have been expressing the most noble and universal sentiment in the dialect of the Cherokees. Objection to the publication of such passages as that, in short, is not the fact that they tell us about the love of the Brownings, but that they do not tell us about it.

Upon this principle it is obvious that there should have been a selection among the Letters, but not a selection which should exclude anything merely because it was ardent and noble. If Browning or Mrs. Browning had not desired any people to know that they were fond of each other, they would not have written and published "One Word More" or "The Sonnets from the Portuguese." Nay, they would not have been married in a public church, for every one who is married in a church does make a confession of love of absolutely national publicity, and tacitly, therefore, repudiates any idea that such confessions are too sacred for the world to know. The ridiculous theory that men should have no noble passions or sentiments in public may have been designed to make private life holy and undefiled, but it has had very little actual effect except to make public life cynical and preposterously unmeaning. But the words of a poem or the words of the English Marriage Service, which are as fine as many poems, is a language dignified and deliberately intended to be understood by all. If the bride and bridegroom in church, instead of uttering those words, were to utter a poem compounded of private allusions to the foibles of Aunt Matilda, or of childish secrets which they would tell each other in a lane, it would be a parallel case to the publication of some of the Browning Letters. Why the serious and universal portions of those Letters could not be published without those which are to us idle and unmeaning it is difficult to understand. Our wisdom, whether expressed in private or public, belongs to the world, but our folly belongs to those we love.

There is at least one peculiarity in the Browning Letters which tends to make their publication far less open to objection than almost any other collection of love letters which can be imagined. The ordinary sentimentalist who delights in the most emotional of magazine interviews, will not be able to get much satisfaction out of them, because he and many persons more acute will be quite unable to make head or tail of three consecutive sentences. In this respect it is the most extraordinary correspondence in the world. There seem to be only two main rules for this form of letter-writing: the first is, that if a sentence can begin with a parenthesis it always should; and the second is, that if you have written from a third to half of a sentence you need never in any case write any more. It would be amusing to watch any one who felt an idle curiosity as to the language and secrets of lovers opening the Browning Letters. He would probably come upon some such simple and lucid passage as the following: "I ought to wait, say a week at least, having killed all your mules for you, before I shot down your dogs. ... But not being exactly Phoibos Apollon, you are to know further that when I *did* think I might go modestly on ... ὤμοι, let me get out of this slough of a simile, never mind with what dislocated ankles."

What our imaginary sentimentalist would make of this tender passage it is difficult indeed to imagine. The only plain conclusion which appears to emerge from the words is the somewhat curious one—that Browning was in the habit of taking a gun down to Wimpole Street and of demolishing the live stock on those somewhat unpromising premises. Nor will he be any better enlightened if he turns to the reply of Miss

Barrett, which seems equally dominated with the great central idea of the Browning correspondence that the most enlightening passages in a letter consist of dots. She replies in a letter following the above: "But if it could be possible that you should mean to say you would show me. . . . Can it be? or am I reading this 'Attic contraction' quite the wrong way. You see I am afraid of the difference between flattering myself and being flattered . . . the fatal difference. And now will you understand that I should be too overjoyed to have revelations from the Portfolio . . . however incarnated with blots and pen scratches . . . to be able to ask impudently of them now? Is that plain?" Most probably she thought it was.

With regard to Browning himself this characteristic is comparatively natural and appropriate. Browning's prose was in any case the most roundabout affair in the world. Those who knew him say that he would often send an urgent telegram from which it was absolutely impossible to gather where the appointment was, or when it was, or what was its object. This fact is one of the best of all arguments against the theory of Browning's intellectual conceit. A man would have to be somewhat abnormally conceited in order to spend sixpence for the pleasure of sending an unintelligible communication to the dislocation of his own plans. The fact was, that it was part of the machinery of his brain that things came out of it, as it were, backwards. The words "tail foremost" express Browning's style with something more than a conventional accuracy. The tail, the most insignificant part of an animal, is also often the most animated and fantastic. An utterance of Browning is often like a strange animal walking backwards, who flourishes his tail with such energy that every one takes it for his head. He was in other words, at least in his prose and practical utterances, more or less incapable of telling a story without telling the least important thing first. If a man who belonged to an Italian secret society, one local branch of which bore as a badge an olive-green ribbon, had entered his house, and in some sensational interview tried to bribe or blackmail him, he would have told the story with great energy and indignation, but he would have been incapable of beginning with anything except the question of the colour of olives. His whole method was founded both in literature and life upon the principle of the "ex pede Herculem," and at the beginning of his description of Hercules the foot appears some sizes larger than the hero. It is, in short, natural enough that Browning should have written his love letters obscurely, since he wrote his letters to his publisher and his solicitor obscurely. In the case of Mrs. Browning it is somewhat more difficult to understand. For she at least had, beyond all question, a quite simple and lucent vein of humour, which does not easily reconcile itself with this subtlety. But she was partly under the influence of her own quality of passionate ingenuity or emotional wit of which we have already taken notice in dealing with her poems, and she was partly also no doubt under the influence of Browning. Whatever was the reason, their correspondence was not of the sort which can be pursued very much by the outside public. Their letters may be published a hundred times over, they still remain private. They write to each other in a language of their own, an almost exasperatingly impressionist language, a language chiefly consisting of dots and dashes and asterisks and italics, and brackets and notes of interrogation. Wordsworth when he heard afterwards of their eventual elopement said with that slight touch of bitterness he always used in speaking of Browning, "So Robert Browning and Miss Barrett have gone off together. I hope they understand each other—nobody else would." It would be difficult to pay a higher compliment to a marriage. Their common affection for Kenyon was a great element in their lives and in their correspondence. "I have a convenient theory to account for Mr. Kenyon," writes Browning mysteriously, "and his otherwise unaccountable kindness to me." "For Mr. Kenyon's kindness," retorts Elizabeth Barrett, "no theory will account. I class it with mesmerism for that reason." There is something very dignified and beautiful about the simplicity of these two poets vying with each other in giving adequate praise to the old dilettante, of whom the world would never have heard but for them. Browning's feeling for him was indeed especially strong and typical. "There," he said, pointing after the old man as he left the room, "there goes one of the most splendid men living—a man so noble in his friendship, so lavish in his hospitality, so large-hearted and benevolent, that he deserves to be known all over the world as 'Kenyon the Magnificent.'" There is something thoroughly worthy of Browning at his best in this feeling, not merely of the use of sociability, or of the charm of sociability, but of the magnificence, the heroic largeness of real sociability. Being himself a warm champion of the pleasures of society, he saw in Kenyon a kind of poetic genius for the thing, a mission of superficial philanthropy. He is thoroughly to be congratulated on the fact that he had grasped the great but now neglected truth, that a man may actually be great, yet not in the least able.

Browning's desire to meet Miss Barrett was received on her side, as has been stated, with a variety of objections. The chief of these was the strangely feminine and irrational reason that she was not worth seeing, a point on which the seeker for an interview might be permitted to form his own opinion. "There is nothing to see in me; nor to hear in me.—I never learned to talk as you do in London; although I can admire that brightness of carved speech in Mr. Kenyon and others. If my poetry is worth anything to any eye, it is the flower of me. I have lived most and been most happy in it, and so it has all my colours; the rest of me is nothing but a root, fit for the ground and dark." The substance of Browning's reply was to the effect, "I will call at two on Tuesday."

They met on May 20, 1845. A short time afterwards he had fallen in love with her and made her an offer of marriage. To a person in the domestic atmosphere of the Barretts, the incident would appear to have been paralysing. "I will tell you what I once said in jest . . ." she writes, "If a prince of El Dorado should come with a pedigree of lineal descent from some signory in the moon in one hand and a ticket of good behaviour from the nearest Independent chapel in the other !—'Why, even *then*,' said my sister Arabel, 'it would not *do*.' And she was right; we all agreed that she was right."

This may be taken as a fairly accurate description of the real state of Mr. Barrett's mind on one subject.

It is illustrative of the very best and breeziest side of Elizabeth Barrett's character that she could be so genuinely humorous over so tragic a condition of the human mind.

Browning's proposals were, of course, as matters stood, of a character to dismay and repel all those who surrounded Elizabeth Barrett. It was not wholly a matter of the fancies of her father. The whole of her family, and most probably the majority of her medical advisers, did seriously believe at this time that she was unfit to be moved, to say nothing of being married, and that a life passed between a bed and a sofa, and avoiding too frequent and abrupt transitions even from one to the other, was the only life she could expect on this earth. Almost alone in holding another opinion and in urging her to a more vigorous view of her condition, stood Browning himself. "But you are better," he would say; "you look so and speak so." Which of the two opinions was right is of course a complex medical matter into which a book like this has neither the right nor the need to enter. But this much may be stated as a mere question of fact. In the summer of 1846 Elizabeth Barrett was still living under the great family convention which provided her with nothing but an elegant deathbed, forbidden to move, forbidden to see proper daylight, forbidden to receive a friend lest the shock should destroy her suddenly. A year or two later, in Italy, as Mrs. Browning, she was being dragged up hill in a wine hamper, toiling up to the crests of mountains at four o'clock in the morning, riding for five miles on a donkey to what she calls "an inaccessible volcanic ground not far from the stars." It is perfectly incredible that any one so ill as her family believed her to be should have lived this life for twenty-four hours. Something must be allowed for the intoxication of a new tie and a new interest in life. But such exaltations can in their nature hardly last a month, and Mrs. Browning lived for fifteen years afterwards in infinitely better health than she had ever known before. In the light of modern knowledge it is not very difficult or very presumptuous, of us to guess that she had been in her father's house to some extent inoculated with hysteria, that strange affliction which some people speak of as if it meant the absence of disease, but which is in truth the most terrible of all diseases. It must be remembered that in 1846 little or nothing was known of spine complaints such as that from which Elizabeth Barrett suffered, less still of the nervous conditions they create, and least of all of hysterical phenomena. In our day she would have been ordered air and sunlight and activity, and all the things the mere idea of which chilled the Barretts with terror. In our day, in short, it would have been recognised that she was in the clutch of a form of neurosis which exhibits every fact of a disease except its origin, that strange possession which makes the body itself a hypocrite. Those who surrounded Miss Barrett knew nothing of this, and Browning knew nothing of it; and probably if he knew anything, knew less than they did. Mrs. Orr says, probably with a great deal of truth, that of ill-health and its sensations he remained "pathetically ignorant" to his dying day. But devoid as he was alike of expert knowledge and personal experience, without a shadow of medical authority, almost without anything that can be formally called a right to his opinion, he was, and remained, right. He at least saw, he indeed alone saw, to the practical centre of the situation. He did not know anything about hysteria or neurosis, or the influence of surroundings, but he knew that the atmosphere of Mr. Barrett's house was not a fit thing for any human being, alive, dying, or dead. His stand upon this matter has really a certain human interest, since it is an example of a thing which will from time to time occur, the interposition of the average man to the confounding of the experts. Experts are undoubtedly right nine times out of ten, but the tenth time comes, and we find in military matters an Oliver Cromwell who will make every mistake known to strategy and yet win all his battles, and in medical matters a Robert Browning whose views have not a technical leg to stand on and are entirely correct.

But while Browning was thus standing alone in his view of the matter, while Edward Barrett had to all appearance on his side a phalanx of all the sanities and respectabilities, there came suddenly a new development, destined to bring matters to a crisis indeed, and to weigh at least three souls in the balance. Upon further examination of Miss Barrett's condition, the physicians had declared that it was absolutely necessary that she should be taken to Italy. This may, without any exaggeration, be called the turning-point and the last great earthly opportunity of Barrett's character. He had not originally been an evil man, only a man who, being stoical in practical things, permitted himself, to his great detriment, a self-indulgence in moral things. He had grown to regard his pious and dying daughter as part of the furniture of the house and of the universe. And as long as the great mass of authorities were on his side, his illusion was quite pardonable. His crisis came when the authorities changed their front, and with one accord asked his permission to send his daughter abroad. It was his crisis, and he refused.

He had, if we may judge from what we know of him, his own peculiar and somewhat detestable way of refusing. Once when his daughter had asked a perfectly simple favour in a matter of expediency, permission, that is, to keep her favourite brother with her during an illness, her singular parent remarked that she might keep him if she liked, but that he had looked for greater self-sacrifice. These were the weapons with which he ruled his people. For the worst tyrant is not the man who rules by fear; the worst tyrant is he who rules by love and plays on it as on a harp. Barrett was one of the oppressors who have discovered the last secret of oppression, that which is told in the fine verse of Swinburne:—

> "The racks of the earth and the rods
> Are weak as the foam on the sands;
> The heart is the prey for the gods,
> Who crucify hearts, not hands."

He, with his terrible appeal to the vibrating consciences of women, was, with regard to one of them, very near to the end of his reign. When Browning heard that the Italian journey was forbidden, he proposed definitely that they should marry and go on the journey together.

Many other persons had taken cognisance of the fact, and were active in the matter. Kenyon, the gentlest and most universally complimentary of mortals, had marched into the house and given Arabella Barrett, the sister of the sick woman, his opinion of her father's conduct with a degree of fire and frankness which must have been perfectly amazing in a man of his almost antiquated social delicacy. Mrs. Jameson, a good and generous friend of the family, had immediately stepped in and offered to take Elizabeth to Italy herself, thus removing all questions of expense or arrangement. She would appear to have stood to her guns in the matter with splendid persistence and magnanimity. She called day after day seeking for a change of mind, and delayed her own journey to the continent more than once. At length, when it became evident that the extraction of Mr. Barrett's consent was hopeless, she reluctantly began her own tour in Europe alone. She went to Paris, and had not been there many days, when she received a formal call from Robert Browning and Elizabeth Barrett Browning, who had been married for some days. Her astonishment is rather a picturesque thing to think about.

The manner in which this sensational elopement, which was, of course, the talk of the whole literary world, had been effected, is narrated, as every one knows, in the Browning Letters. Browning had decided that an immediate marriage was the only solution; and having put his hand to the plough, did not decline even when it became obviously necessary that it should be a secret marriage. To a man of his somewhat stormily candid and casual disposition this necessity of secrecy was really exasperating; but every one with any imagination or chivalry will rejoice that he accepted the evil conditions. He had always had the courage to tell the truth; and now it was demanded of him to have the greater courage to tell a lie, and he told it with perfect cheerfulness and lucidity. In thus disappearing surreptitiously with an invalid woman he was doing something against which there were undoubtedly a hundred things to be said, only it happened that the most cogent and important thing of all was to be said for it.

It is very amusing, and very significant in the matter of Browning's character, to read the accounts which he writes to Elizabeth Barrett of his attitude towards the approaching *coup de théâtre*. In one place he says, suggestively enough, that he does not in the least trouble about the disapproval of her father; the man whom he fears as a frustrating influence is Kenyon. Mr. Barrett could only walk into the room and fly into a passion; and this Browning could have received with perfect equanimity. But, he says, if Kenyon knows of the matter, I shall have the kindest and friendliest of explanations (with his arm on my shoulder) of how I am ruining your social position, destroying your health, etc., etc. This touch is very suggestive of the power of the old worldling, who could manœuvre with young people as well as Major Pendennis. Kenyon had indeed long been perfectly aware of the way in which things were going; and the method he adopted in order to comment on it is rather entertaining. In a conversation with Elizabeth Barrett, he asked carelessly whether there was anything between her sister and a certain Captain Cooke, and remarked apologetically that he had been led into the idea by the gentleman calling so often at the house. Elizabeth Barrett knew perfectly well what he meant; but the logical allusiveness of the attack reminds one of a fragment of some Meredithian comedy.

The manner in which Browning bore himself in this acute and necessarily dubious position is, perhaps, more thoroughly to his credit than anything else in his career. He never came out so well in all his long years of sincerity and publicity as he does in this one act of deception. Having made up his mind to that act, he is not ashamed to name it; neither, on the other hand, does he rant about it, and talk about Philistine prejudices and higher laws and brides in the sight of God, after the manner of the cockney decadent. He was breaking a social law, but he was not declaring a crusade against social laws. We all feel, whatever may be our opinions on the matter, that the great danger of this kind of social opportunism, this pitting of a private necessity against a public custom, is that men are somewhat too weak and self-deceptive to be trusted with such a power of giving dispensations to themselves. We feel that men without meaning to do so might easily begin by breaking a social by-law and end by being thoroughly anti-social. One of the best and most striking things to notice about Robert Browning is the fact that he did this thing considering it as an exception, and that he contrived to leave it really exceptional. It did not in the least degree break the rounded clearness of his loyalty to social custom. It did not in the least degree weaken the sanctity of the general rule. At a supreme crisis of his life he did an unconventional thing, and he lived and died conventional. It would be hard to say whether he appears the more thoroughly sane in having performed the act, or in not having allowed it to affect him.

Elizabeth Barrett gradually gave way under the obstinate and almost monotonous assertion of Browning

that this elopement was the only possible course of
action. Before she finally agreed, however, she did
something, which in its curious and impulsive symbolism, belongs almost to a more primitive age. The
sullen system of medical seclusion to which she had
long been subjected has already been described. The
most urgent and hygienic changes were opposed by
many on the ground that it was not safe for her to leave
her sofa and her sombre room. On the day on which
it was necessary for her finally to accept or reject
Browning's proposal, she called her sister to her, and
to the amazement and mystification of that lady asked
for a carriage. In this she drove into Regent's Park,
alighted, walked on to the grass, and stood leaning
against a tree for some moments, looking round
her at the leaves and the sky. She then entered
the carriage again, drove home, and agreed to the
elopement. This was possibly the best poem that she
ever produced.

Browning arranged the eccentric adventure with a
great deal of prudence and knowledge of human nature.
Early one morning in September 1846 Miss Barrett
walked quietly out of her father's house, became Mrs.
Robert Browning in a church in Marylebone, and
returned home again as if nothing had happened. In
this arrangement Browning showed some of that real
insight into the human spirit which ought to make
a poet the most practical of all men. The incident
was, in the nature of things, almost overpoweringly
exciting to his wife, in spite of the truly miraculous
courage with which she supported it; and he desired,
therefore, to call in the aid of the mysteriously tranquillising effect of familiar scenes and faces. One

trifling incident is worth mentioning which is almost unfathomably characteristic of Browning. It has already been remarked in these pages that he was preeminently one of those men whose expanding opinions never alter by a hairsbreadth the actual ground-plan of their moral sense. Browning would have felt the same things right and the same things wrong, whatever views he had held. During the brief and most trying period between his actual marriage and his actual elopement, it is most significant that he would not call at the house in Wimpole Street, because he would have been obliged to ask if Miss Barrett was disengaged. He was acting a lie; he was deceiving a father; he was putting a sick woman to a terrible risk; and these things he did not disguise from himself for a moment, but he could not bring himself to say two words to a maidservant. Here there may be partly the feeling of the literary man for the sacredness of the uttered word, but there is far more of a certain rooted traditional morality which it is impossible either to describe or to justify. Browning's respectability was an older and more primeval thing than the oldest and most primeval passions of other men. If we wish to understand him, we must always remember that in dealing with any of his actions we have not to ask whether the action contains the highest morality, but whether we should have felt inclined to do it ourselves.

At length the equivocal and exhausting interregnum was over. Mrs. Browning went for the second time almost on tiptoe out of her father's house, accompanied only by her maid and her dog, which was only just successfully prevented from barking. Before the end of the day in all probability Barrett had discovered that his dying daughter had fled with Browning to Italy.

They never saw him again, and hardly more than a faint echo came to them of the domestic earthquake which they left behind them. They do not appear to have had many hopes, or to have made many attempts at a reconciliation. Elizabeth Barrett had discovered at last that her father was in truth not a man to be treated with; hardly, perhaps, even a man to be blamed. She knew to all intents and purposes that she had grown up in the house of a madman.

CHAPTER IV

BROWNING IN ITALY

THE married pair went to Pisa in 1846, and moved soon afterwards to Florence. Of the life of the Brownings in Italy there is much perhaps to be said in the way of description and analysis, little to be said in the way of actual narrative. Each of them had passed through the one incident of existence. Just as Elizabeth Barrett's life had before her marriage been uneventfully sombre, now it was uneventfully happy. A succession of splendid landscapes, a succession of brilliant friends, a succession of high and ardent intellectual interests, they experienced; but their life was of the kind that if it were told at all, would need to be told in a hundred volumes of gorgeous intellectual gossip. How Browning and his wife rode far into the country, eating strawberries and drinking milk out of the basins of the peasants; how they fell in with the strangest and most picturesque figures of Italian society; how they climbed mountains and read books and modelled in clay and played on musical instruments; how Browning was made a kind of arbiter between two improvising Italian bards; how he had to escape from a festivity when the sound of Garibaldi's hymn brought the knocking of the Austrian police; these are the things of which his life is full, trifling and picturesque things, a series of interludes, a beautiful and happy story, beginning and ending nowhere. The only incidents, perhaps, were the birth of their son and the death of Browning's mother in 1849.

It is well known that Browning loved Italy; that it was his adopted country; that he said in one of the finest of his lyrics that the name of it would be found written on his heart. But the particular character of this love of Browning for Italy needs to be understood. There are thousands of educated Europeans who love Italy, who live in it, who visit it annually, who come across a continent to see it, who hunt out its darkest picture and its most mouldering carving; but they are all united in this, that they regard Italy as a dead place. It is a branch of their universal museum, a department of dry bones. There are rich and cultivated persons, particularly Americans, who seem to think that they keep Italy, as they might keep an aviary or a hothouse, into which they might walk whenever they wanted a whiff of beauty. Browning did not feel at all in this manner; he was intrinsically incapable of offering such an insult to the soul of a nation. If he could not have loved Italy as a nation, he would not have consented to love it as an old curiosity shop. In everything on earth, from the Middle Ages to the amœba, who is discussed at such length in "Mr. Sludge the Medium," he is interested in the life in things. He was interested in the life in Italian art and in the life in Italian politics.

Perhaps the first and simplest example that can be given of this matter is in Browning's interest in art. He was immeasurably fascinated at all times by painting and sculpture, and his sojourn in Italy gave him, of course, innumerable and perfect opportunities for the study of painting and sculpture. But his interest in these studies was not like that of the ordinary cultured visitor to the Italian cities. Thousands of such visitors, for example, study those endless lines of magnificent Pagan busts which are to be found in nearly all the Italian galleries and museums, and admire them, and talk about them, and note them in their catalogues, and describe them in their diaries. But the way in which they affected Browning is described very suggestively in a passage in the letters of his wife. She describes herself as longing for her husband to write poems, beseeching him to write poems, but finding all her petitions useless because her husband was engaged all day in modelling busts in clay and breaking them as fast as he made them. This is Browning's interest in art, the interest in a living thing, the interest in a growing thing, the insatiable interest in how things are done. Every one who knows his admirable poems on painting—"Fra Lippo Lippi" and "Andrea del Sarto" and "Pictor Ignotus"—will remember how fully they deal with technicalities, how they are concerned with canvas, with oil, with a mess of colours. Sometimes they are so technical as to be mysterious to the casual reader. An extreme case may be found in that of a lady I once knew who had merely read the title of "Pacchiarotto and how he worked in distemper," and thought that Pacchiarotto was the name of a dog, whom no attacks of canine disease could keep from the fulfilment of his duty. These Browning poems do not merely deal with painting; they smell of paint. They are the works of a man to whom art is not what it is to so many of the non-professional lovers of art, a thing accomplished, a valley of bones: to him it is a field of crops continually growing in a busy and exciting silence. Browning was interested, like some scientific man, in the obstetrics of art. There is a large army of educated men who can talk art with artists; but Browning could not merely talk art with artists—he could talk shop with them. Personally he may not have known enough about painting to be more than a fifth-rate painter, or enough about the organ to be more than a sixth-rate organist. But there are, when all is said and done, some things which a fifth-rate painter knows which a first-rate art critic does not know; there are some things which a sixth-rate organist knows which a first-rate judge of music does not know. And these were the things that Browning knew.

He was, in other words, what is called an amateur. The word amateur has come by the thousand oddities of language to convey an idea of tepidity; whereas the word itself has the meaning of passion. Nor is this peculiarity confined to the mere form of the word; the actual characteristic of these nameless dilettanti is a genuine fire and reality. A man must love a thing very much if he not only practises it without any hope of fame or money, but even practises it without any hope of doing it well. Such a man must love the toils of the work more than any other man can love the rewards of it. Browning was in this strict sense a strenuous amateur. He tried and practised in the course of his life half a hundred things at which he can never have even for a moment expected to succeed. The story of his life is full of absurd little ingenuities, such as the discovery of a way of making pictures by

smoking paper over a candle. In precisely the same
spirit of fruitless vivacity, he made himself to a very
considerable extent a technical expert in painting, a
technical expert in sculpture, a technical expert in
music. In his old age, he shows traces of being so
bizarre a thing as an abstract police detective, writing
at length in letters and diaries his views of certain
criminal cases in an Italian town. Indeed, his own
Ring and the Book is merely a sublime detective story.
He was in a hundred things this type of man; he
was precisely in the position, with a touch of greater
technical success, of the admirable figure in Stevenson's
story who said, "I can play the fiddle nearly well
enough to earn a living in the orchestra of a penny
gaff, but not quite."

The love of Browning for Italian art, therefore, was
anything but an antiquarian fancy; it was the love of
a living thing. We see the same phenomenon in an
even more important matter—the essence and individuality of the country itself.

Italy to Browning and his wife was not by any
means merely that sculptured and ornate sepulchre
that it is to so many of those cultivated English men
and women who live in Italy and enjoy and admire
and despise it. To them it was a living nation, the
type and centre of the religion and politics of a continent; the ancient and flaming heart of Western
history, the very Europe of Europe. And they lived
at the time of the most moving and gigantic of all
dramas—the making of a new nation, one of the things
that makes men feel that they are still in the morning
of the earth. Before their eyes, with every circumstance of energy and mystery, was passing the panorama

of the unification of Italy, with the bold and romantic militarism of Garibaldi, the more bold and more romantic diplomacy of Cavour. They lived in a time when affairs of State had almost the air of works of art; and it is not strange that these two poets should have become politicians in one of those great creative epochs when even the politicians have to be poets.

Browning was on this question and on all the questions of continental and English politics a very strong Liberal. This fact is not a mere detail of purely biographical interest, like any view he might take of the authorship of the "Eikon Basilike" or the authenticity of the Tichborne claimant. Liberalism was so inevitably involved in the poet's whole view of existence, that even a thoughtful and imaginative Conservative would feel that Browning was bound to be a Liberal. His mind was possessed, perhaps even to excess, by a belief in growth and energy and in the ultimate utility of error. He held the great central Liberal doctrine, a belief in a certain destiny of the human spirit beyond, and perhaps even independent of, our own sincerest convictions. The world was going right he felt, most probably in his way, but certainly in its own way. The sonnet which he wrote in later years, entitled "Why I am a Liberal," expresses admirably this philosophical root of his politics. It asks in effect how he, who had found truth in so many strange forms after so many strange wanderings, can be expected to stifle with horror the eccentricities of others. A Liberal may be defined approximately as a man who, if he could by waving his hand in a dark room, stop the mouths of all the deceivers of mankind for ever, would not wave his hand. Browning was a Liberal in this sense.

And just as the great Liberal movement which followed the French Revolution made this claim for the liberty and personality of human beings, so it made it for the liberty and personality of nations. It attached indeed to the independence of a nation something of the same wholly transcendental sanctity which humanity has in all legal systems attached to the life of a man. The grounds were indeed much the same; no one could say absolutely that a live man was useless, and no one could say absolutely that a variety of national life was useless or must remain useless to the world. Men remembered how often barbarous tribes or strange and alien Scriptures had been called in to revive the blood of decaying empires and civilisations. And this sense of the personality of a nation, as distinct from the personalities of all other nations, did not involve in the case of these old Liberals international bitterness; for it is too often forgotten that friendship demands independence and equality fully as much as war. But in them it led to great international partialities, to a great system, as it were, of adopted countries which made so thorough a Scotchman as Carlyle in love with Germany, and so thorough an Englishman as Browning in love with Italy.

And while on the one side of the struggle was this great ideal of energy and variety, on the other side was something which we now find it difficult to realise or describe. We have seen in our own time a great reaction in favour of monarchy, aristocracy, and ecclesiasticism, a reaction almost entirely noble in its instinct, and dwelling almost entirely on the best periods and the best qualities of the old *régime*. But the modern man, full of admiration for the great virtue of chivalry which is at the heart of aristocracies, and the great virtue of reverence which is at the heart of ceremonial religion, is not in a position to form any idea of how profoundly unchivalrous, how astonishingly irreverent, how utterly mean, and material, and devoid of mystery or sentiment were the despotic systems of Europe which survived, and for a time conquered, the Revolution. The case against the Church in Italy in the time of Pio Nono was not the case which a rationalist would urge against the Church of the time of St. Louis, but diametrically the opposite case. Against the mediæval Church it might be said that she was too fantastic, too visionary, too dogmatic about the destiny of man, too indifferent to all things but the devotional side of the soul. Against the Church of Pio Nono the main thing to be said was that it was simply and supremely cynical; that it was not founded on the unworldly instinct for distorting life, but on the worldly counsel to leave life as it is; that it was not the inspirer of insane hopes, of reward and miracle, but the enemy, the cool and sceptical enemy, of hope of any kind or description. The same was true of the monarchical systems of Prussia and Austria and Russia at this time. Their philosophy was not the philosophy of the cavaliers who rode after Charles I. or Louis XIII. It was the philosophy of the typical city uncle, advising every one, and especially the young, to avoid enthusiasm, to avoid beauty, to regard life as a machine, dependent only upon the two forces of comfort and fear. That was, there can be little doubt, the real reason of the fascination of the Napoleon legend—that while Napoleon was a despot like the rest, he was a despot who went somewhere and did something, and defied the pessimism of Europe, and erased the word "impossible." One does not need to be a Bonapartist to rejoice at the way in which the armies of the First Empire, shouting their songs and jesting with their colonels, smote and broke into pieces the armies of Prussia and Austria driven into battle with a cane.

Browning, as we have said, was in Italy at the time of the break-up of one part of this frozen continent of the non-possumus. Austria's hold in the north of Italy was part of that elaborate and comfortable and wholly cowardly and unmeaning compromise, which the Holy Alliance had established, and which it believed without doubt in its solid unbelief would last until the Day of Judgment, though it is difficult to imagine what the Holy Alliance thought would happen then. But almost of a sudden affairs had begun to move strangely, and the despotic princes and their chancellors discovered with a great deal of astonishment that they were not living in the old age of the world, but to all appearance in a very unmanageable period of its boyhood. In an age of ugliness and routine, in a time when diplomatists and philosophers alike tended to believe that they had a list of all human types, there began to appear men who belonged to the morning of the world, men whose movements have a national breadth and beauty, who act symbols and become legends while they are alive. Garibaldi in his red shirt rode in an open carriage along the front of a hostile fort calling to the coachman to drive slower, and not a man dared fire a shot at him. Mazzini poured out upon Europe a new mysticism of humanity and liberty, and was willing, like some passionate Jesuit of the sixteenth century, to become in its cause either a philosopher or a criminal. Cavour arose with a diplomacy which was more thrilling and picturesque than war itself. These men had nothing to do with an age of the impossible. They have passed, their theories along with them, as all things pass; but since then we have had no men of their type precisely, at once large and real and romantic and successful. Gordon was a possible exception. They were the last of the heroes.

When Browning was first living in Italy, a telegram which had been sent to him was stopped on the frontier and suppressed on account of his known sympathy with the Italian Liberals. It is almost impossible for people living in a commonwealth like ours to understand how a small thing like that will affect a man. It was not so much the obvious fact that a great practical injury was really done to him; that the telegram might have altered all his plans in matters of vital moment. It was, over and above that, the sense of a hand laid on something personal and essentially free. Tyranny like this is not the worst tyranny, but it is the most intolerable. It interferes with men not in the most serious matters, but precisely in those matters in which they most resent interference. It may be illogical for men to accept cheerfully unpardonable public scandals, benighted educational systems, bad sanitation, bad lighting, a blundering and inefficient system of life, and yet to resent the tearing up of a telegram or a postcard; but the fact remains that the sensitiveness of men is a strange and localised thing, and there is hardly a man in the world who would not rather be ruled by despots chosen by lot and live in a city like a mediæval

Ghetto, than be forbidden by a policeman to smoke another cigarette, or sit up a quarter of an hour later; hardly a man who would not feel inclined in such a case to raise a rebellion for a caprice for which he did not really care a straw. Unmeaning and muddle-headed tyranny in small things, that is the thing which, if extended over many years, is harder to bear and hope through than the massacres of September. And that was the nightmare of vexatious triviality which was lying over all the cities of Italy that were ruled by the bureaucratic despotisms of Europe. The history of the time is full of spiteful and almost childish struggles—struggles about the humming of a tune or the wearing of a colour, the arrest of a journey, or the opening of a letter. And there can be little doubt that Browning's temperament under these conditions was not of the kind to become more indulgent, and there grew in him a hatred of the Imperial and Ducal and Papal systems of Italy, which sometimes passed the necessities of Liberalism, and sometimes even transgressed its spirit. The life which he and his wife lived in Italy was extraordinarily full and varied, when we consider the restrictions under which one at least of them had always lain. They met and took delight, notwithstanding their exile, in some of the most interesting people of their time—Ruskin, Cardinal Manning, and Lord Lytton. Browning, in a most characteristic way, enjoyed the society of all of them, arguing with one, agreeing with another, sitting up all night by the bedside of a third.

It has frequently been stated that the only difference that ever separated Mr. and Mrs. Browning was upon the question of spiritualism. That statement must, of course, be modified and even contradicted if it means that they never differed; that Mr. Browning never thought an Act of Parliament good when Mrs. Browning thought it bad; that Mr. Browning never thought bread stale when Mrs. Browning thought it new. Such unanimity is not only inconceivable, it is immoral; and as a matter of fact, there is abundant evidence that their marriage constituted something like that ideal marriage, an alliance between two strong and independent forces. They differed, in truth, about a great many things, for example, about Napoleon III. whom Mrs. Browning regarded with an admiration which would have been somewhat beyond the deserts of Sir Galahad, and whom Browning with his emphatic Liberal principles could never pardon for the *Coup d'État*. If they differed on spiritualism in a somewhat more serious way than this, the reason must be sought in qualities which were deeper and more elemental in both their characters than any mere matter of opinion. Mrs. Orr, in her excellent *Life of Browning*, states that the difficulty arose from Mrs. Browning's firm belief in psychical phenomena and Browning's absolute refusal to believe even in their possibility. Another writer who met them at this time says, "Browning cannot believe, and Mrs. Browning cannot help believing." This theory, that Browning's aversion to the spiritualist circle arose from an absolute denial of the tenability of such a theory of life and death, has in fact often been repeated. But it is exceedingly difficult to reconcile it with Browning's character. He was the last man in the world to be intellectually deaf to a hypothesis merely because it was odd. He had friends whose opinions covered every description of madness from the French legitimism of De Ripert-Monclar to the Republicanism of Landor. Intellectually he may be said to have had a zest for heresies. It is difficult to impute an attitude of mere impenetrable negation to a man who had expressed with sympathy the religion of "Caliban" and the morality of "Time's Revenges." It is true that at this time of the first popular interest in spiritualism a feeling existed among many people of a practical turn of mind, which can only be called a superstition against believing in ghosts. But, intellectually speaking, Browning would probably have been one of the most tolerant and curious in regard to the new theories, whereas the popular version of the matter makes him unusually intolerant and negligent even for that time. The fact was in all probability that Browning's aversion to the spiritualists had little or nothing to do with spiritualism. It arose from quite a different side of his character—his uncompromising dislike of what is called Bohemianism, of eccentric or slovenly cliques, of those straggling camp followers of the arts who exhibit dubious manners and dubious morals, of all abnormality and of all irresponsibility. Any one, in fact, who wishes to see what it was that Browning disliked need only do two things. First, he should read the *Incidents of my Life*, by Daniel Home, the famous spiritualist medium with whom Browning came in contact. These *Incidents* constitute a more thorough and artistic self-revelation than any monologue that Browning ever wrote. The ghosts, the raps, the flying hands, the phantom voices are infinitely the most respectable and infinitely the most credible part of the narrative. But the bragging, the sentimentalism, the moral and intellectual foppery of the composition is everywhere, culminating perhaps in the disgusting passage in which Home describes Mrs. Browning as weeping over him, and assuring him that all her husband's actions in the matter have been adopted against her will. It is in this kind of thing that we find the roots of the real anger of Browning. He did not dislike spiritualism, but spiritualists. The second point on which any one wishing to be just in the matter should cast an eye, is the record of the visit which Mrs. Browning insisted on making while on their honeymoon in Paris to the house of George Sand. Browning felt, and to some extent expressed, exactly the same aversion to his wife mixing with the circle of George Sand which he afterwards felt at her mixing with the circle of Home. The society was "of the ragged red, diluted with the low theatrical, men who worship George Sand, *à genoux bas* between an oath and an ejection of saliva." When we find that a man did not object to any number of Jacobites or Atheists, but objected to the French Bohemian poets and to the early occultist mediums as friends for his wife, we shall surely be fairly right in concluding that he objected not to an opinion, but to a social tone. The truth was that Browning had a great many admirably Philistine feelings, and one of them was a great relish for his responsibilities towards his wife. He enjoyed being a husband. This is quite a distinct thing from enjoying being a lover, though it will scarcely be found apart from it. But, like all good feelings, it has its possible exaggerations, and one of them is this almost morbid healthiness in the choice of friends for his wife.

Daniel Home, the medium, came to Florence about 1857. Mrs. Browning undoubtedly threw herself into psychical experiments with great ardour at first, and

Browning, equally undoubtedly, opposed, and at length forbade, the enterprise. He did not do so however until he had attended one *séance* at least, at which a somewhat ridiculous event occurred, which is described in Home's Memoirs with a gravity even more absurd than the incident. Towards the end of the proceedings a wreath was placed in the centre of the table, and the lights being lowered, it was caused to rise slowly into the air, and after hovering for some time, to move towards Mrs. Browning, and at length to alight upon her head. As the wreath was floating in her direction, her husband was observed abruptly to cross the room and stand beside her. One would think it was a sufficiently natural action on the part of a man whose wife was the centre of a weird and disturbing experiment, genuine or otherwise. But Mr. Home gravely asserts that it was generally believed that Browning had crossed the room in the hope that the wreath would alight on his head, and that from the hour of its disobliging refusal to do so dated the whole of his goaded and malignant aversion to spiritualism. The idea of the very conventional and somewhat bored Robert Browning running about the room after a wreath in the hope of putting his head into it, is one of the genuine gleams of humour in this rather foolish affair. Browning could be fairly violent, as we know, both in poetry and conversation; but it would be almost too terrible to conjecture what he would have felt and said if Mr. Home's wreath had alighted on his head.

Next day, according to Home's account, he called on the hostess of the previous night, pallid with rage and behaving like a maniac, and told her apparently that she must excuse him if he and his wife did not attend any more gatherings of the kind. What actually occurred is not, of course, quite easy to ascertain, for the account in Home's Memoirs principally consists of noble speeches made by the medium which would seem either to have reduced Browning to a pulverised silence, or else to have failed to attract his attention. But there can be no doubt that the general upshot of the affair was that Browning put his foot down, and the experiments ceased. There can be little doubt that he was justified in this; indeed, he was probably even more justified if the experiments were genuine psychical mysteries than if they were the *hocus-pocus* of a charlatan. He knew his wife better than posterity can be expected to do; but even posterity can see that she was the type of woman so much adapted to the purposes of men like Home as to exhibit almost invariably either a great craving for such experiences or a great terror of them. Like many geniuses, but not all, she lived naturally upon something like a borderland; and it is impossible to say that if Browning had not interposed when she was becoming hysterical she might not have ended in an asylum.

The whole of this incident is very characteristic of Browning; but the real characteristic note in it has, as above suggested, been to some extent missed. When some seven years afterwards he produced "Mr. Sludge the Medium," every one supposed that it was an attack upon spiritualism and the possibility of its phenomena. As we shall see when we come to that poem, this is a wholly mistaken interpretation of it. But what is really curious is that most people have assumed that a dislike of Home's investigations implies a theoretic disbelief in spiritualism. It might, of course, imply a very firm and serious belief in it. As a matter of fact it did not imply this in Browning, but it may perfectly well have implied an agnosticism which admitted the reasonableness of such things. Home was infinitely less dangerous as a dexterous swindler than he was as a bad or foolish man in possession of unknown or ill-comprehended powers. It is surely curious to think that a man must object to exposing his wife to a few conjuring tricks, but could not be afraid of exposing her to the loose and nameless energies of the universe.

Browning's theoretic attitude in the matter was, therefore, in all probability quite open and unbiassed. His was a peculiarly hospitable intellect. If any one had told him of the spiritualist theory, or theories a hundred times more insane, as things held by some sect of Gnostics in Alexandria, or of heretical Talmudists at Antwerp, he would have delighted in those theories, and would very likely have adopted them. But Greek Gnostics and Antwerp Jews do not dance round a man's wife and wave their hands in her face and send her into swoons and trances about which nobody knows anything rational or scientific. It was simply the stirring in Browning of certain primal masculine feelings far beyond the reach of argument—things that lie so deep that if they are hurt, though there may be no blame and no anger, there is always pain. Browning did not like spiritualism to be mentioned for many years.

Robert Browning was unquestionably a thoroughly conventional man. There are many who think this element of conventionality altogether regrettable and disgraceful; they have established, as it were, a convention of the unconventional. But this hatred of the conventional element in the personality of a poet is only possible to those who do not remember the meaning of words. Convention means only a coming together, an agreement; and as every poet must base his work upon an emotional agreement among men, so every poet must base his work upon a convention. Every art is, of course, based upon a convention, an agreement between the speaker and the listener that certain objections shall not be raised. The most realistic art in the world is open to realistic objection. Against the most exact and everyday drama that ever came out of Norway it is still possible for the realist to raise the objection that the hero who starts a subject and drops it, who runs out of a room and runs back again for his hat, is all the time behaving in a most eccentric manner, considering that he is doing these things in a room in which one of the four walls has been taken clean away and been replaced by a line of footlights and a mob of strangers. Against the most accurate black-and-white artist that human imagination can conceive it is still to be admitted that he draws a black line round a man's nose, and that that line is a lie. And in precisely the same fashion a poet must, by the nature of things, be conventional. Unless he is describing an emotion which others share with him, his labours will be utterly in vain. If a poet really had an original emotion; if, for example, a poet suddenly fell in love with the buffers of a railway train, it would take him considerably more time than his allotted three-score years and ten to communicate his feelings.

Poetry deals with primal and conventional things—the hunger for bread, the love of woman, the love of children, the desire for immortal life. If men really had new sentiments, poetry could not deal with them. If, let us say, a man did not feel a bitter craving to eat bread; but did, by way of substitute, feel a fresh, original craving to eat brass fenders or mahogany tables, poetry could not express him. If a man, instead of falling in love with a woman, fell in love with a fossil or a sea anemone, poetry could not express him. Poetry can only express what is original in one sense—the sense in which we speak of original sin. It is original, not in the paltry sense of being new, but in the deeper sense of being old; it is original in the sense that it deals with origins.

All artists, who have any experience of the arts, will agree so far, that a poet is bound to be conventional with regard to matters of art. Unfortunately, however, they are the very people who cannot, as a general rule, see that a poet is also bound to be conventional in matters of conduct. It is only the smaller poet who sees the poetry of revolt, of isolation, of disagreement; the larger poet sees the poetry of those great agreements which constitute the romantic achievement of civilisation. Just as an agreement between the dramatist and the audience is necessary to every play; just as an agreement between the painter and the spectators is necessary to every picture, so an agreement is necessary to produce the worship of any of the great figures of morality—the hero, the saint, the average man, the gentleman. Browning had, it must thoroughly be realised, a real pleasure in these great agreements, these great conventions. He delighted, with a true poetic delight, in being conventional. Being by birth an Englishman, he took pleasure in being an Englishman; being by rank a member of the middle class, he took a pride in its ancient scruples and its everlasting boundaries. He was everything that he was with a definite and conscious pleasure—a man, a Liberal, an Englishman, an author, a gentleman, a lover, a married man.

This must always be remembered as a general characteristic of Browning, this ardent and headlong conventionality. He exhibited it pre-eminently in the affair of his elopement and marriage, during and after the escape of himself and his wife to Italy. He seems to have forgotten everything, except the splendid worry of being married. He showed a thoroughly healthy consciousness that he was taking up a responsibility which had its practical side. He came finally and entirely out of his dreams. Since he had himself enough money to live on, he had never thought of himself as doing anything but writing poetry; poetry indeed was probably simmering and bubbling in his head day and night. But when the problem of the elopement arose he threw himself with an energy, of which it is pleasant to read, into every kind of scheme for solidifying his position. He wrote to Monckton Milnes, and would appear to have badgered him with applications for a post in the British Museum. "I will work like a horse," he said, with that boyish note, which, whenever in his unconsciousness he strikes it, is more poetical than all his poems. All his language in this matter is emphatic; he would be "glad and proud," he says, "to have any minor post" his friend could obtain for him. He offered to read for the Bar, and probably began doing so. But all this vigorous and very creditable materialism was ruthlessly extinguished by Elizabeth Barrett. She declined altogether even to entertain the idea of her husband devoting himself to anything else at the expense of poetry. Probably she was right and Browning wrong, but it was an error which every man would desire to have made.

One of the qualities again which make Browning most charming, is the fact that he felt and expressed so simple and genuine a satisfaction about his own achievements as a lover and husband, particularly in relation to his triumph in the hygienic care of his wife. "If he is vain of anything," writes Mrs. Browning, "it is of my restored health." Later, she adds with admirable humour and suggestiveness, "and I have to tell him that he really must not go telling everybody how his wife walked here with him, or walked there with him, as if a wife with two feet were a miracle in Nature." When a lady in Italy said, on an occasion when Browning stayed behind with his wife on the day of a picnic, that he was "the only man who behaved like a Christian to his wife," Browning was elated to an almost infantile degree. But there could scarcely be a better test of the essential manliness and decency of a man than this test of his vanities. Browning boasted of being domesticated; there are half a hundred men everywhere who would be inclined to boast of not being domesticated. Bad men are almost without exception conceited, but they are commonly conceited of their defects.

One picturesque figure who plays a part in this portion of the Brownings' life in Italy is Walter Savage Landor. Browning found him living with some of his wife's relations, and engaged in a continuous and furious quarrel with them, which was, indeed, not uncommonly the condition of that remarkable man when living with other human beings. He had the double arrogance which is only possible to that old and stately but almost extinct blend—the aristocratic republican. Like an old Roman senator, or like a gentleman of the Southern States of America, he had the condescension of a gentleman to those below him, combined with the jealous self-assertiveness of a Jacobin to those above. The only person who appears to have been able to manage him and bring out his more agreeable side was Browning. It is, by the way, one of the many hints of a certain element in Browning which can only be described by the elementary and old-fashioned word goodness, that he always contrived to make himself acceptable and even lovable to men of savage and capricious temperament, of detached and erratic genius, who could get on with no one else. Carlyle, who could not get a bitter taste off his tongue in talking of most of his contemporaries, was fond of Browning. Landor, who could hardly conduct an ordinary business interview without beginning to break the furniture, was fond of Browning. These are things which speak more for a man than many people will understand. It is easy enough to be agreeable to a circle of admirers, especially feminine admirers, who have a peculiar talent for discipleship and the absorption of ideas. But when a man is loved by other men of his own intellectual stature and of a wholly different type and order of eminence, we may be certain that there was something genuine about him, and something far more important than anything intellectual. Men do not like another man because he is a genius, least of all when they happen to be geniuses themselves. This general truth about Browning is like hearing of a woman who is the most famous beauty in a city, and who is at the same time adored and confided in by all the women who live there.

Browning came to the rescue of the fiery old gentleman, and helped by Seymour Kirkup put him under very definite obligations by a course of very generous conduct. He was fully repaid in his own mind for his trouble by the mere presence and friendship of Landor, for whose quaint and volcanic personality he had a vast admiration, compounded of the pleasure of the artist in an oddity and of the man in a hero. It is somewhat amusing and characteristic that Mrs. Browning did not share this unlimited enjoyment of the company of Mr. Landor, and expressed her feelings in her own humorous manner. She writes, "Dear, darling Robert amuses me by talking of his gentleness and sweetness. A most courteous and refined gentleman he is, of course, and very affectionate to Robert (as he ought to be), but of self-restraint he has not a grain, and of suspicion many grains. What do you really say to dashing down a plate on the floor when you don't like what's on it? Robert succeeded in soothing him, and the poor old lion is very quiet on the whole, roaring softly to beguile the time in Latin alcaics against his wife and Louis Napoleon."

One event alone could really end this endless life of the Italian Arcadia. That event happened on June 29, 1861. Robert Browning's wife died, stricken by the death of her sister, and almost as hard (it is a characteristic touch) by the death of Cavour. She died alone in the room with Browning, and of what passed then, though much has been said, little should be. He, closing the door of that room behind him, closed a door in himself, and none ever saw Browning upon earth again but only a splendid surface.

CHAPTER V

BROWNING IN LATER LIFE

BROWNING'S confidences, what there were of them, immediately after his wife's death were given to several women-friends; all his life, indeed, he was chiefly intimate with women. The two most intimate of these were his own sister, who remained with him in all his later years, and the sister of his wife, who seven years afterwards passed away in his presence as Elizabeth had done. The other letters, which number only one or two, referring in any personal manner to his bereavement are addressed to Miss Haworth and Isa Blagden. He left Florence and remained for a time with his father and sister near Dinard. Then he returned to London and took up his residence in Warwick Crescent. Naturally enough, the thing for which he now chiefly lived was the education of his son, and it is characteristic of Browning that he was not only a very indulgent father, but an indulgent father of a very conventional type: he had rather the chuckling pride of the city gentleman than the educational gravity of the intellectual.

Browning was now famous. *Bells and Pomegranates*, *Men and Women*, *Christmas Eve*, and *Dramatis Personæ* had successively glorified his Italian period. But he was already brooding half-unconsciously on more famous things. He has himself left on record a description of the incident out of which grew the whole impulse and plan of his greatest achievement. In a passage marked with all his peculiar sense of material things, all that power of writing of stone or metal or the fabric of drapery, so that we seem to be handling and smelling them, he has described a stall for the selling of odds and ends of every variety of utility and uselessness:—

> "picture frames
> White through the worn gilt, mirror-sconces chipped,
> Bronze angel-heads once knobs attached to chests,
> (Handled when ancient dames chose forth brocade)
> Modern chalk drawings, studies from the nude,
> Samples of stone, jet, breccia, porphyry
> Polished and rough, sundry amazing busts
> In baked earth, (broken, Providence be praised!)
> A wreck of tapestry proudly-purposed web
> When reds and blues were indeed red and blue,
> Now offer'd as a mat to save bare feet
> (Since carpets constitute a cruel cost).
> * * * * * *
> Vulgarised Horace for the use of schools,
> 'The Life, Death, Miracles of Saint Somebody,
> Saint Somebody Else, his Miracles, Death, and Life —
> With this, one glance at the lettered back of which,
> And 'Stall,' cried I; a *lira* made it mine."

This sketch embodies indeed the very poetry of *débris*, and comes nearer than any other poem has done to expressing the pathos and picturesqueness of a low-class pawnshop. "This," which Browning bought for a lira out of this heap of rubbish, was, of course, the old Latin record of the criminal case of Guido Franceschini, tried for the murder of his wife Pompilia in the year 1698. And this again, it is scarcely necessary to say, was the ground-plan and motive of *The Ring and the Book*.

Browning had picked up the volume and partly planned the poem during his wife's lifetime in Italy. But the more he studied it, the more the dimensions of the theme appeared to widen and deepen; and he came at last, there can be little doubt, to regard it definitely as his *magnum opus* to which he would devote many years to come. Then came the great sorrow of his life, and he cast about him for something sufficiently immense and arduous and complicated to keep his brain going like some huge and automatic engine. "I mean to keep writing," he said, "whether I like it or not." And thus finally he took up the scheme of the Franceschini story, and developed it on a scale with a degree of elaboration, repetition, and management, and inexhaustible scholarship which was never perhaps before given in the history of the world to an affair of two or three characters. Of the larger literary and spiritual significance of the work, particularly in reference to its curious and original form of narration, I shall speak subsequently. But there is one peculiarity about the story which has more direct bearing on Browning's life, and it appears singular that few, if any, of his critics have noticed it. This peculiarity is the extraordinary resemblance between the moral problem involved in the poem if understood in its essence, and the moral problem which constituted the crisis and centre of Browning's own life. Nothing, properly speaking, ever happened to Browning after his wife's death; and his greatest work during that time was the telling, under alien symbols and the veil of a wholly different story, the inner truth about his own greatest trial and hesitation. He himself had in this sense the same difficulty as Caponsacchi, the supreme difficulty of having to trust himself to the reality of virtue not only without the reward, but even without the name of virtue. He had, like Caponsacchi, preferred what was unselfish and dubious to what was selfish and honourable. He knew better than any man that there is little danger of men who really know anything of that naked and homeless responsibility seeking it too often or indulging it too much. The conscientiousness of the law-abider is nothing in its terrors to the conscientiousness of the conscientious law-breaker. Browning had once, for what he seriously believed to be a greater good, done what he himself would never have had the cant to deny, ought to be called deceit and evasion. Such a thing ought never to come to a man twice. If he finds that necessity twice, he may, I think, be looked at with the beginning of a suspicion. To Browning it came once, and he devoted his greatest poem to a suggestion of how such a necessity may come to any man who is worthy to live.

As has already been suggested, any apparent danger that there may be in this excusing of an exceptional act is counteracted by the perils of the act, since it must always be remembered that this kind of act has the immense difference from all legal acts—that it can only be justified by success. If Browning had taken his wife to Paris, and she had died in an hotel there, we can only conceive him saying, with the bitter emphasis of one of his own lines, "How should I have borne me, please?" Before and after this event his life was as tranquil and casual a one as it would be easy to imagine; but there always remained upon him something which was felt by all who knew him in after years—the spirit of a man who had been ready when his time came, and had walked in his own devotion and certainty in a position counted indefensible and almost along the brink of murder. This great moral of Browning, which may be called roughly the doctrine of the great hour, enters, of course, into many poems besides *The Ring and the Book*, and is indeed the mainspring of a great part of his poetry taken as a whole. It is, of course, the central idea of that fine poem, "The Statue and the Bust," which has given a great deal of distress to a great many people because of its supposed invasion of recognised morality. It deals, as every one knows, with a Duke Ferdinand and an elopement which he planned with the bride of one of the Riccardi. The lovers begin by deferring their flight for various more or less comprehensible reasons of convenience; but the habit of shrinking from the final step grows steadily upon them, and they never take it, but die, as it were, waiting for each other. The objection that the act thus avoided was a criminal one is very simply and quite clearly answered by Browning himself. His case against the dilatory couple is not in the least affected by the viciousness of their aim. His case is that they exhibited no virtue. Crime was frustrated in them by cowardice, which is probably the worse immorality of the two. The same idea again may be found in that delightful lyric "Youth and Art," where a successful cantatrice reproaches a successful sculptor with their failure to understand each other in their youth and poverty.

> "Each life unfulfilled, you see;
> It hangs still, patchy and scrappy:
> We have not sighed deep, laughed free,
> Starved, feasted, despaired,—been happy."

And this conception of the great hour, which breaks out everywhere in Browning, it is almost impossible not to connect with his own internal drama. It is really curious that this correspondence has not been insisted on. Probably critics have been misled by the fact that Browning in many places appears to boast that he is purely dramatic, that he has never put himself into his work, a thing which no poet, good or bad, who ever lived could possibly avoid doing.

The enormous scope and seriousness of *The Ring and the Book* occupied Browning for some five or six years, and the great epic appeared in the winter of 1868. Just before it was published Smith and Elder brought out a uniform edition of all Browning's works up to that time, and the two incidents taken together may be considered to mark the final and somewhat belated culmination of Browning's literary fame. The years since his wife's death, that had been covered by the writing of *The Ring and the Book*, had been years of an almost feverish activity in that and many other ways. His travels had been restless and continued, his industry immense, and for the first time he began that mode of life which afterwards became so characteristic of him— the life of what is called society. A man of a shallower and more sentimental type would have professed to find the life of dinner-tables and soirées vain and unsatisfying to a poet, and especially to a poet in mourning. But if there is one thing more than another which is stirring and honourable about Browning, it is the entire absence in him of this cant of dissatisfaction. He had the one great requirement of a poet—he was not difficult to please. The life of society was superficial, but it is only very superficial people who object to the superficial. To the man who sees the marvellousness of all things, the surface of life is fully as strange and magical as its interior; clearness and plainness of life is fully as mysterious as its mysteries. The young man in evening dress, pulling on his gloves, is quite as elemental a figure as any anchorite, quite as incomprehensible, and indeed quite as alarming.

A great many literary persons have expressed astonishment at, or even disapproval of, this social frivolity of Browning's. Not one of these literary people would have been shocked if Browning's interest in humanity had led him into a gambling hell in the Wild West or a low tavern in Paris; but it seems to be tacitly assumed that fashionable people are not human at all. Humanitarians of a material and dogmatic type, the philanthropists and the professional reformers go to look for humanity in remote places and in huge statistics. Humanitarians of a more vivid type, the Bohemian artists, go to look for humanity in thieves' kitchens and the studios of the Quartier Latin. But humanitarians of the highest type, the great poets and philosophers, do not go to look for humanity at all. For them alone among all men the nearest drawing-room is full of humanity, and even their own families are human. Shakespeare ended his life by buying a house in his own native town and talking to the townsmen. Browning was invited to a great many conversaziones and private views, and did not pretend that they bored him. In a letter belonging to this period of his life he describes his first dinner at one of the Oxford colleges with an unaffected delight and vanity, which reminds the reader of nothing so much as the pride of the boy-captain of a public school if he were invited to a similar function and received a few compliments. It may be indeed that Browning had a kind of second youth in this long-delayed social recognition, but at least he enjoyed his second youth nearly as much as his first, and it is not every one who can do that.

Of Browning's actual personality and presence in this later middle age of his, memories are still sufficiently clear. He was a middle-sized, well set up, erect man, with somewhat emphatic gestures, and, as almost all testimonies mention, a curiously strident voice. The beard, the removal of which his wife had resented with so quaint an indignation, had grown again, but grown quite white, which, as she said when it occurred, was a signal mark of the justice of the gods. His hair was still fairly dark, and his whole appearance at this time must have been very well represented by Mr. G. F. Watts's fine portrait in the National Portrait Gallery. The portrait bears one of the many testimonies which exist to Mr. Watts's grasp of the essential of character, for it is the only one of the portraits of Browning in which we get primarily the air of virility, even of animal virility, tempered but not disguised, with a certain touch of the pallor of the brain-worker. He looks here what he was—a very healthy man, too scholarly to live a completely healthy life.

His manner in society, as has been more than once indicated, was that of a man anxious, if anything, to avoid the air of intellectual eminence. Lockhart said briefly, "I like Browning; he isn't at all like a damned literary man." He was, according to some, upon occasion, talkative and noisy to a fault; but there are two kinds of men who monopolise conversation. The first kind are those who like the sound of their own voice; the second are those who do not know what the sound of their own voice is like. Browning was one of the latter class. His volubility in speech had the same origin as his voluminousness and obscurity in literature—a kind of headlong humility. He cannot assuredly have been aware that he talked people down or have wished to do so. For this would have been precisely a violation of the ideal of the man of the world, the one ambition and even weakness that he had. He wished to be a man of the world, and he never in the full sense was one. He remained a little too much of a boy, a little too much even of a Puritan, and a little too much of what may be called a man of the universe, to be a man of the world.

One of his faults probably was the thing roughly called prejudice. On the question, for example, of table-turning and psychic phenomena he was in a certain degree fierce and irrational. He was not indeed, as we shall see when we come to study "Sludge the Medium," exactly prejudiced against spiritualism. But he was beyond all question stubbornly prejudiced against spiritualists. Whether the medium Home was or was not a scoundrel it is somewhat difficult in our day to conjecture. But in so far as he claimed supernatural powers, he may have been as honest a gentleman as ever lived. And even if we think that the moral atmosphere of Home is that of a man of dubious character, we can still feel that

Browning might have achieved his purpose without making it so obvious that he thought so. Some traces again, though much fainter ones, may be found of something like a subconscious hostility to the Roman Church, or at least a less full comprehension of the grandeur of the Latin religious civilisation than might have been expected of a man of Browning's great imaginative tolerance. Æstheticism, Bohemianism, the irresponsibilities of the artist, the untidy morals of Grub Street and the Latin Quarter, he hated with a consuming hatred. He was himself exact in everything, from his scholarship to his clothes; and even when he wore the loose white garments of the lounger in Southern Europe, they were in their own way as precise as a dress suit. This extra carefulness in all things he defended against the cant of Bohemianism as the right attitude for the poet. When some one excused coarseness or negligence on the ground of genius, he said, "That is an error: Noblesse oblige."

Browning's prejudices, however, belonged altogether to that healthy order which is characterised by a cheerful and satisfied ignorance. It never does a man any very great harm to hate a thing that he knows nothing about. It is the hating of a thing when we do know something about it which corrodes the character. We all have a dark feeling of resistance towards people we have never met, and a profound and manly dislike of the authors we have never read. It does not harm a man to be certain before opening the books that Whitman is an obscene ranter or that Stevenson is a mere trifler with style. It is the man who can think these things after he has read the books who must be in a fair way to mental perdition. Prejudice, in fact, is not so much the great intellectual sin as a thing which we may call, to coin a word, "postjudice," not the bias before the fair trial, but the bias that remains afterwards. With Browning's swift and emphatic nature the bias was almost always formed before he had gone into the matter. But almost all the men he really knew he admired, almost all the books he had really read he enjoyed. He stands pre-eminent among those great universalists who praised the ground they trod on and commended existence like any other material, in its samples. He had no kinship with those new and strange universalists of the type of Tolstoi who praise existence to the exclusion of all the institutions they have lived under, and all the ties they have known. He thought the world good because he had found so many things that were good in it—religion, the nation, the family, the social class. He did not, like the new humanitarian, think the world good because he had found so many things in it that were bad.

As has been previously suggested, there was something very queer and dangerous that underlay all the good humour of Browning. If one of these idle prejudices were broken by better knowledge, he was all the better pleased. But if some of the prejudices that were really rooted in him were trodden on, even by accident, such as his aversion to loose artistic cliques, or his aversion to undignified publicity, his rage was something wholly transfiguring and alarming, something far removed from the shrill disapproval of Carlyle and Ruskin. It can only be said that he became a savage, and not always a very agreeable or presentable savage. The indecent fury which danced upon the bones of Edward Fitzgerald was a thing which ought not to have astonished any one who had known much of Browning's character or even of his work. Some unfortunate persons on another occasion had obtained some of Mrs. Browning's letters shortly after her death, and proposed to write a *Life* founded upon them. They ought to have understood that Browning would probably disapprove; but if he talked to them about it, as he did to others, and it is exceedingly probable that he did, they must have thought he was mad. "What I suffer with the paws of these blackguards in my bowels you can fancy," he says. Again he writes: "Think of this beast working away, not deeming my feelings, or those of her family, worthy of notice. It shall not be done if I can stop the scamp's knavery along with his breath." Whether Browning actually resorted to this extreme course is unknown; nothing is known except that he wrote a letter to the ambitious biographer which reduced him to silence, probably from stupefaction.

The same peculiarity ought, as I have said, to have been apparent to any one who knew anything of Browning's literary work. A great number of his poems are marked by a trait of which by its nature it is more or less impossible to give examples. Suffice it to say that it is truly extraordinary that poets like Swinburne (who seldom uses a gross word) should have been spoken of as if they had introduced moral license into Victorian poetry. What the Nonconformist conscience has been doing to have passed Browning is something difficult to imagine. But the peculiarity of this occasional coarseness in his work is this—that it is always used to express a certain wholesome fury and contempt for things sickly, or ungenerous, or unmanly. The poet seems to feel that there are some things so contemptible that you can only speak of them in pothouse words. It would be idle, and perhaps undesirable, to give examples; but it may be noted that the same brutal physical metaphor is used by his Caponsacchi about the people who could imagine Pompilia impure and by his Shakespeare in "At the Mermaid," about the claim of the Byronic poet to enter into the heart of humanity. In both cases Browning feels, and perhaps in a manner rightly, that the best thing we can do with a sentiment essentially base is to strip off its affectations and state it basely, and that the mud of Chaucer is a great deal better than the poison of Sterne. Herein again Browning is close to the average man; and to do the average man justice, there is a great deal more of this Browningesque hatred of Byronism in the brutality of his conversation than many people suppose.

Such, roughly and as far as we can discover, was the man who, in the full summer and even the full autumn of his intellectual powers, began to grow upon the consciousness of the English literary world about this time. For the first time friendship grew between him and the other great men of his time. Tennyson, for whom he then and always felt the best and most personal kind of admiration, came into his life, and along with him Gladstone and Francis Palgrave. There began to crowd in upon him those honours whereby a man is to some extent made a classic in his lifetime, so that he is honoured even if he is unread. He was made a Fellow of Balliol in 1867, and the homage of the great universities continued thenceforth unceasingly until his death, despite many refusals on his part. He was twice asked to be a candidate for the Lord Rectorship of Glasgow University. He declined, owing to his deep and somewhat characteristic aversion to formal public speaking, and in 1877 he had to decline on similar grounds the similar invitation from the University of St. Andrews. He was much at the English universities, was a friend of Dr. Jowett, and enjoyed the university life at the age of sixty-three in a way that he probably would not have enjoyed it if he had ever been to a university. The great universities would not let him alone, to their great credit, and he became a D.C.L. of Cambridge in 1879, and a D.C.L. of Oxford in 1882. When he received these honours there were, of course, the traditional buffooneries of the undergraduates, and one of them dropped a red cotton night-cap neatly on his head as he passed under the gallery. Some indignant intellectuals wrote to him to protest against this affront, but Browning took the matter in the best and most characteristic way. "You are far too hard," he wrote in answer, "on the very harmless drolleries of the young men. Indeed, there used to be a regularly appointed jester, 'Filius Terrae' he was called, whose business it was to gibe and jeer at the honoured ones by way of reminder that all human glories are merely gilded baubles and must not be fancied metal." In this there are other and deeper things characteristic of Browning besides his learning and humour. In discussing anything, he must always fall back upon great speculative and eternal ideas. Even in the tomfoolery of a horde of undergraduates he can only see a symbol of the ancient office of ridicule in the scheme of morals. The young men themselves were probably unaware that they were the representatives of the "Filius Terrae."

But the years during which Browning was thus reaping some of his late laurels began to be filled with incidents that reminded him how the years were passing over him. On June 20, 1866, his father had died, a man of whom it is impossible to think without a certain emotion, a man who had lived quietly and persistently for others, to whom Browning owed more than it is easy to guess, to whom we in all probability mainly owe Browning. In 1868 one of his closest friends, Arabella Barrett, the sister of his wife, died, as her sister had done, alone with Browning. Browning was not a superstitious man; he somewhat stormily prided himself on the contrary; but he notes at this time "a dream which Arabella had of Her, in which she prophesied their meeting in five years," that is, of course, the meeting of Elizabeth and Arabella. His friend Milsand, to whom *Sordello* was dedicated, died in 1886. "I never knew," said Browning, "or ever shall know, his like among men." But though both fame and a growing isolation indicated that he was passing towards the evening of his days, though he bore traces of the progress, in a milder attitude towards things, and a greater preference for long exiles with those he loved, one thing continued in him with unconquerable energy —there was no diminution in the quantity, no abatement in the immense designs of his intellectual output.

In 1871 he produced *Balaustion's Adventure*, a work exhibiting not only his genius in its highest condition of power, but something more exacting even than genius to a man of his mature and changed life, immense investigation, prodigious memory, the thorough assimilation of the vast literature of a remote civilisation. *Balaustion's Adventure*, which is, of course, the mere framework for an English version of the Alcestis of Euripides, is an illustration of one of Browning's finest traits, his immeasurable capacity for a classic admiration. Those who knew him tell us that in conversation he never revealed himself so impetuously or so brilliantly as when declaiming the poetry of others; and *Balaustion's Adventure* is a monument of this fiery self-forgetfulness. It is penetrated with the passionate desire to render Euripides worthily, and to that imitation are for the time being devoted all the gigantic powers which went to make the songs of Pippa and the last agony of Guido. Browning never put himself into anything more powerfully or more successfully; yet it is only an excellent translation. In the uncouth philosophy of Caliban, in the tangled ethics of Sludge, in his wildest satire, in his most feather-headed lyric, Browning was never more thoroughly Browning than in this splendid and unselfish plagiarism. This revived excitement in Greek matters; "his passionate love of the Greek language" continued in him thenceforward till his death. He published more than one poem on the drama of Hellas. *Aristophanes' Apology* came out in 1875, and *The Agamemnon of Æschylus*, another paraphrase, in 1877. All three poems are marked by the same primary characteristic, the fact that the writer has the literature of Athens literally at his fingers' ends. He is intimate not only with their poetry and politics, but with their frivolity and their slang; he knows not only Athenian wisdom, but Athenian folly; not only the beauty of Greece, but even its vulgarity. In fact, a page of *Aristophanes' Apology* is like a page of

Aristophanes, dark with levity and as obscure as a schoolman's treatise, with its load of jokes.

In 1871 also appeared *Prince Hohenstiel-Schwangau: Saviour of Society*, one of the finest and most picturesque of all Browning's apologetic monologues. The figure is, of course, intended for Napoleon III., whose Empire had just fallen, bringing down his country with it. The saying has been often quoted that Louis Napoleon deceived Europe twice—once when he made it think he was a noodle, and once when he made it think he was a statesman. It might be added that Europe was never quite just to him, and was deceived a third time, when it took him after his fall for an exploded mountebank and nonentity. Amid the general chorus of contempt which was raised over his weak and unscrupulous policy in later years, culminating in his great disaster, there are few things finer than this attempt of Browning's to give the man a platform and let him speak for himself. It is the apologia of a political adventurer, and a political adventurer of a kind peculiarly open to popular condemnation. Mankind has always been somewhat inclined to forgive the adventurer who destroys or re-creates, but there is nothing inspiring about the adventurer who merely preserves. We have sympathy with the rebel who aims at reconstruction, but there is something repugnant to the imagination in the rebel who rebels in the name of compromise. Browning had to defend, or rather to interpret, a man who kidnapped politicians in the night and deluged the Montmartre with blood, not for an ideal, not for a reform, not precisely even for a cause, but simply for the establishment of a *régime*. He did these hideous things not so much that he might be able to do better ones, but that he and every one else might be able to do nothing for twenty years; and Browning's contention, and a very plausible contention, is that the criminal believed that his crime would establish order and compromise, or, in other words, that he thought that nothing was the very best thing he and his people could do. There is something peculiarly characteristic of Browning in thus selecting not only a political villain, but what would appear the most prosaic kind of villain. We scarcely ever find in Browning a defence of those obvious and easily defended publicans and sinners whose mingled virtues and vices are the stuff of romance and melodrama— the generous rake, the kindly drunkard, the strong man too great for parochial morals. He was in a yet more solitary sense the friend of the outcast. He took in the sinners whom even sinners cast out. He went with the hypocrite and had mercy on the Pharisee.

How little this desire of Browning's, to look for a moment at the man's life with the man's eyes, was understood, may be gathered from the criticisms on *Hohenstiel-Schwangau*, which, says Browning, "the Editor of the *Edinburgh Review* calls my eulogium on the Second Empire, which it is not, any more than what another wiseacre affirms it to be, a scandalous attack on the old constant friend of England. It is just what I imagine the man might, if he pleased, say for himself."

In 1873 appeared *Red-Cotton Night-Cap Country*, which, if it be not absolutely one of the finest of Browning's poems, is certainly one of the most magnificently Browningesque. The origin of the name of the poem is probably well known. He was travelling along the Normandy coast, and discovered what he called

> "Meek, hitherto un-Murrayed bathing-place,
> Best loved of sea-coast-nook-ful Normandy!"

Miss Thackeray, who was of the party, delighted Browning beyond measure by calling the sleepy old fishing district "White Cotton Night-Cap Country." It was exactly the kind of elfish phrase to which Browning had, it must always be remembered, a quite unconquerable attraction. The notion of a town of sleep, where men and women walked about in nightcaps, a nation of somnambulists, was the kind of thing that Browning in his heart loved better than *Paradise Lost*. Some time afterwards he read in a newspaper a very painful story of profligacy and suicide which greatly occupied the French journals in the year 1871, and which had taken place in the same district. It is worth noting that Browning was one of those wise men who can perceive the terrible and impressive poetry of the police-news, which is commonly treated as vulgarity, which is dreadful and may be undesirable, but is certainly not vulgar. From *The Ring and the Book* to *Red-Cotton Night-Cap Country* a great many of his works might be called magnificent detective stories. The story is somewhat ugly, and its power does not alter its ugliness, for power can only make ugliness uglier. And in this poem there is little or nothing of the revelation of that secret wealth of valour and patience in humanity which makes real and redeems the revelation of its secret vileness in *The Ring and the Book*. It almost looks at first sight as if Browning had for a moment surrendered the whole of his impregnable philosophical position and admitted the strange heresy that a human story can be sordid. But this view of the poem is, of course, a mistake. It was written in something which, for want of a more exact word, we must call one of the bitter moods of Browning; but the bitterness is entirely the product of a certain generous hostility against the class of morbidities which he really detested, sometimes more than they deserved. In this poem these principles of weakness and evil are embodied to him as the sicklier kind of Romanism, and the more sensual side of the French temperament. We must never forget what a great deal of the Puritan there remained in Browning to the end. This outburst of it is fierce and ironical, not in his best spirit. It says in effect, "You call this a country of sleep, I call it a country of death. You call it 'White Cotton Night-Cap Country'; I call it 'Red Cotton Night-Cap Country.'"

Shortly before this, in 1872, he had published *Fifine at the Fair*, which his principal biographer, and one of his most uncompromising admirers, calls a piece of perplexing cynicism. Perplexing it may be to some extent, for it was almost impossible to tell whether Browning would or would not be perplexing even in a love-song or a post-card. But cynicism is a word that cannot possibly be applied with any propriety to anything that Browning ever wrote. Cynicism denotes that condition of mind in which we hold that life is in its nature mean and arid; that no soul contains genuine goodness, and no state of things genuine reliability. *Fifine at the Fair*, like *Prince Hohenstiel-Schwangau*, is one of Browning's apologetic soliloquies

—the soliloquy of an epicurean who seeks half-playfully to justify upon moral grounds an infidelity into which he afterwards actually falls. This casuist, like all Browning's casuists, is given many noble outbursts and sincere moments, and therefore apparently the poem is called cynical. It is difficult to understand what particular connection there is between seeing good in nobody and seeing good even in a sensual fool.

After *Fifine at the Fair* appeared the *Inn Album*, in 1875, a purely narrative work, chiefly interesting as exhibiting in yet another place one of Browning's vital characteristics, a pleasure in retelling and interpreting actual events of a sinister and criminal type; and after the *Inn Album* came what is perhaps the most preposterously individual thing he ever wrote, *Of Pacchiarotto, and How He Worked in Distemper*, in 1876. It is impossible to call the work poetry, and it is very difficult indeed to know what to call it. Its chief characteristic is a kind of galloping energy, an energy that has nothing intellectual or even intelligible about it, a purely animal energy of words. Not only is it not beautiful, it is not even clever, and yet it carries the reader away as he might be carried away by romping children. It ends up with a voluble and largely unmeaning malediction upon the poet's critics, a malediction so outrageously good-humoured that it does not take the trouble even to make itself clear to the objects of its wrath. One can compare the poem to nothing in heaven or earth, except to the somewhat humorous, more or less benevolent, and most incomprehensible catalogues of curses and oaths which may be heard from an intoxicated navvy. This is the kind of thing, and it goes on for pages :—

"Long after the last of your number
  Has ceased my front-court to encumber
While, treading down rose and ranunculus,
You *Tommy-make-room-for-your-uncle*-us!
Troop, all of you man or homunculus,
Quick march! for Xanthippe, my housemaid,
If once on your pates she a souse made
With what, pan or pot, bowl or *skoramis*,
First comes to her hand—things were more amiss!
I would not for worlds be your place in—
Recipient of slops from the basin!
You, Jack-in-the-Green, leaf-and-twiggishness
Won't save a dry thread on your priggishness!"

You can only call this, in the most literal sense of the word, the brute-force of language.

In spite however of this monstrosity among poems, which gives its title to the volume, it contains some of the most beautiful verses that Browning ever wrote in that style of light philosophy in which he was unequalled. Nothing ever gave so perfectly and artistically what is too loosely talked about as a thrill, as the poem called "Fears and Scruples," in which a man describes the mystifying conduct of an absent friend, and reserves to the last line the climax—

"Hush, I pray you!
What if this friend happen to be—God."

It is the masterpiece of that excellent but much-abused literary quality, Sensationalism.

The volume entitled *Pacchiarotto*, moreover, includes one or two of the most spirited poems on the subject of the poet in relation to publicity—"At the Mermaid," "House," and "Shop."

In spite of his increasing years, his books seemed

if anything to come thicker and faster. Two were published in 1878—*La Saisiaz*, his great metaphysical poem on the conception of immortality, and that delightfully foppish fragment of the *ancien régime*, *The Two Poets of Croisic*. Those two poems would alone suffice to show that he had not forgotten the hard science of theology or the harder science of humour. Another collection followed in 1879, the first series of *Dramatic Idylls*, which contain such masterpieces as "Pheidippides" and "Ivàn Ivànovitch." Upon its heels, in 1880, came the second series of *Dramatic Idylls*, including "Muléykeh" and "Clive," possibly the two best stories in poetry, told in the best manner of story-telling. Then only did the marvellous fountain begin to slacken in quantity, but never in quality. *Jocoseria* did not appear till 1883. It contains among other things a cast-back to his very earliest manner in the lyric of "Never the Time and the Place," which we may call the most light-hearted love-song that was ever written by a man over seventy. In the next year appeared *Ferishtah's Fancies*, which exhibit some of his shrewdest cosmic sagacity, expressed in some of his quaintest and most characteristic images. Here perhaps more than anywhere else we see that supreme peculiarity of Browning—his sense of the symbolism of material trifles. Enormous problems, and yet more enormous answers, about pain, prayer, destiny, liberty, and conscience are suggested by cherries, by the sun, by a melon-seller, by an eagle flying in the sky, by a man tilling a plot of ground. It is this spirit of grotesque allegory which really characterises Browning among all other poets. Other poets might possibly have hit upon the same philosophical idea—some idea as deep, as delicate, and as spiritual. But it may be safely asserted that no other poet, having thought of a deep, delicate, and spiritual idea, would call it "A Bean Stripe; also Apple Eating."

Three more years passed, and the last book which Browning published in his lifetime was *Parleyings with Certain People of Importance in their Day*, a book which consists of apostrophes, amicable, furious, reverential, satirical, emotional to a number of people of whom the vast majority even of cultivated people have never heard in their lives—Daniel Bartoli, Francis Furini, Gerard de Lairesse, and Charles Avison. This extraordinary knowledge of the fulness of history was a thing which never ceased to characterise Browning even when he was unfortunate in every other literary quality. Apart altogether from every line he ever wrote, it may fairly be said that no mind so rich as his ever carried its treasures to the grave. All these later poems are vigorous, learned, and full-blooded. They are thoroughly characteristic of their author. But nothing in them is quite so characteristic of their author as this fact, that when he had published all of them, and was already near to his last day, he turned with the energy of a boy let out of school, and began, of all things in the world, to re-write and improve "Pauline," the boyish poem that he had written fifty-five years before. Here was a man covered with glory and near to the doors of death, who was prepared to give himself the elaborate trouble of reconstructing the mood, and rebuilding the verses of a long juvenile poem which had been forgotten for fifty years in the blaze of successive victories. It is such things as these which give to Browning an interest of personality which is far beyond the mere interest of genius. It was of such things that Elizabeth Barrett wrote in one of her best moments of insight—that his genius was the least important thing about him.

During all these later years, Browning's life had been a quiet and regular one. He always spent the winter in Italy and the summer in London, and carried his old love of precision to the extent of never failing day after day throughout the year to leave the house at the same time. He had by this time become far more of a public figure than he had ever been previously, both in England and Italy. In 1881, Dr. Furnivall and Miss E. H. Hickey founded the famous "Browning Society." He became President of the new "Shakespeare Society" and of the "Wordsworth Society." In 1886, on the death of Lord Houghton, he accepted the post of Foreign Correspondent to the Royal Academy. When he moved to De Vere Gardens in 1887, it began to be evident that he was slowly breaking up. He still dined out constantly; he still attended every reception and private view; he still corresponded prodigiously, and even added to his correspondence; and there is nothing more typical of him than that now, when he was almost already a classic, he answered any compliment with the most delightful vanity and embarrassment. In a letter to Mr. George Bainton, touching style, he makes a remark which is an excellent criticism on his whole literary career: "I myself found many forgotten fields which have proved the richest of pastures." But despite his continued energy, his health was gradually growing worse. He was a strong man in a muscular, and ordinarily in a physical sense, but he was also in a certain sense a nervous man, and may be said to have died of brain-excitement prolonged through a lifetime. In these closing years he began to feel more constantly the necessity for rest. He and his sister went to live at a little hotel in Llangollen, and spent hours together talking and drinking tea on the lawn. He himself writes in one of his quaint and poetic phrases that he had come to love these long country retreats, "another term of delightful weeks, each tipped with a sweet starry Sunday at the little church." For the first time, and in the last two or three years, he was really growing old. On one point he maintained always a tranquil and unvarying decision. The pessimistic school of poetry was growing up all round him; the decadents, with their belief that art was only a counting of the autumn leaves, were approaching more and more towards their tired triumph and their tasteless popularity. But Browning would not for one instant take the scorn of them out of his voice. "Death, death, it is this harping on death that I despise so much. In fiction, in poetry, French as well as English, and I am told in American also, in art and literature, the shadow of death, call it what you will, despair, negation, indifference, is upon us. But what fools who talk thus! Why, *amico mio*, you know as well as I, that death is life, just as our daily momentarily dying body is none the less alive, and ever recruiting new forces of existence. Without death, which is our church-yardy crape-like word for change, for growth, there could be no prolongation of that which we call life. Never say of me that I am dead."

On August 13, 1888, he set out once more for Italy, the last of his innumerable voyages. During his last Italian period he seems to have fallen back on very ultimate simplicities, chiefly a mere staring at nature. The family with whom he lived kept a fox cub, and Browning would spend hours with it watching its grotesque ways; when it escaped, he was characteristically enough delighted. The old man could be seen continually in the lanes round Asolo, peering into hedges and whistling for the lizards.

This serene and pastoral decline, surely the mildest of slopes into death, was suddenly diversified by a flash of something lying far below. Browning's eye fell upon a passage written by the distinguished Edward Fitzgerald, who had been dead for many years, in which Fitzgerald spoke in an uncomplimentary manner of Elizabeth Barrett Browning. Browning immediately wrote the "Lines to Edward Fitzgerald," and set the whole literary world in an uproar. The lines were bitter and excessive to have been written against any man, especially bitter and excessive to have been written against a man who was not alive to reply. And yet, when all is said, it is impossible not to feel a certain dark and indescribable pleasure in this last burst of the old barbaric energy. The mountain had been tilled and forested, and laid out in gardens to the summit; but for one last night it had proved itself once more a volcano, and had lit up all the plains with its forgotten fire. And the blow, savage as it was, was dealt for that great central sanctity—the story of a man's youth. All that the old man would say in reply to every view of the question was, "I felt as if she had died yesterday."

Towards December of 1889 he moved to Venice, where he fell ill. He took very little food; it was indeed one of his peculiar small fads that men should not take food when they are ill, a matter in which he maintained that the animals were more sagacious. He asserted vigorously that this somewhat singular regimen would pull him through, talked about his plans, and appeared cheerful. Gradually, however, the talking became more infrequent, the cheerfulness passed into a kind of placidity; and without any particular crisis or sign of the end, Robert Browning died on December 12, 1889. The body was taken on board ship by the Venice Municipal Guard, and received by the Royal Italian marines. He was buried in the Poets' Corner of Westminster Abbey, the choir singing his wife's poem, "He giveth His beloved sleep." On the day that he died *Asolando* was published.

CHAPTER VI

BROWNING AS A LITERARY ARTIST

Mr. William Sharp, in his *Life* of Browning, quotes the remarks of another critic to the following effect: "The poet's processes of thought are scientific in their precision and analysis; the sudden conclusion that he imposes upon them is transcendental and inept."

This is a very fair but a very curious example of the way in which Browning is treated. For what is the state of affairs? A man publishes a series of poems, vigorous, perplexing, and unique. The critics read them, and they decide that he has failed as a poet, but that he is a remarkable philosopher and logician. They then proceed to examine his philosophy, and show with great triumph that it is unphilosophical, and to examine his logic and show with great triumph that it is not logical, but "transcendental and inept." In other words, Browning is first denounced for being a logician and not a poet, and then denounced for insisting on being a poet when they have decided that he is to be a logician. It is just as if a man were to say first that a garden was so neglected that it was only fit for a boys' playground, and then complain of the unsuitability in a boys' playground of rockeries and flower-beds.

As we find, after this manner, that Browning does

not act satisfactorily as that which we have decided that he shall be—a logician—it might possibly be worth while to make another attempt to see whether he may not, after all, be more valid than we thought as to what he himself professed to be—a poet. And if we study this seriously and sympathetically, we shall soon come to a conclusion. It is a gross and complete slander upon Browning to say that his processes of thought are scientific in their precision and analysis. They are nothing of the sort; if they were, Browning could not be a good poet. The critic speaks of the conclusions of a poem as "transcendental and inept"; but the conclusions of a poem, if they are not transcendental, must be inept. Do the people who call one of Browning's poems scientific in its analysis realise the meaning of what they say? One is tempted to think that they know a scientific analysis when they see it as little as they know a good poem. The one supreme difference between the scientific method and the artistic method is, roughly speaking, simply this—that a scientific statement means the same thing wherever and whenever it is uttered, and that an artistic statement means something entirely different, according to the relation in which it stands to its surroundings. The remark, let us say, that the whale is a mammal, or the remark that sixteen ounces go to a pound, is equally true, and means exactly the same thing, whether we state it at the beginning of a conversation or at the end, whether we print it in a dictionary or chalk it up on a wall. But if we take some phrase commonly used in the art of literature—such a sentence, for the sake of example, as "the dawn was breaking"—the matter is quite different. If the sentence came at the beginning of a short story, it might be a mere descriptive prelude. If it were the last sentence in a short story, it might be poignant with some peculiar irony or triumph. Can any one read Browning's great monologues and not feel that they are built up like a good short story, entirely on this principle of the value of language arising from its arrangement. Take such an example as "Caliban upon Setebos," a wonderful poem designed to describe the way in which a primitive nature may at once be afraid of its gods and yet familiar with them. Caliban in describing his deity starts with a more or less natural and obvious parallel between the deity and himself, carries out the comparison with consistency and an almost revolting simplicity, and ends in a kind of blasphemous extravaganza of anthropomorphism, basing his conduct not merely on the greatness and wisdom, but also on the manifest weaknesses and stupidities, of the Creator of all things. Then suddenly a thunderstorm breaks over Caliban's island, and the profane speculator falls flat upon his face—

> "Lo! 'Lieth flat and loveth Setebos!
> 'Maketh his teeth meet through his upper lip,
> Will let those quails fly, will not eat this month
> One little mess of whelks, so he may 'scape!"

Surely it would be very difficult to persuade oneself that this thunderstorm would have meant exactly the same thing if it had occurred at the beginning of "Caliban upon Setebos." It does not mean the same thing, but something very different; and the deduction from this is the curious fact that Browning is an artist, and that consequently his processes of thought are not "scientific in their precision and analysis."

No criticism of Browning's poems can be vital, none in the face of the poems themselves can be even intelligible, which is not based upon the fact that he was successfully or otherwise a conscious and deliberate artist. He may have failed as an artist, though I do not think so; that is quite a different matter. But it is one thing to say that a man through vanity or ignorance has built an ugly cathedral, and quite another to say that he built it in a fit of absence of mind, and did not know whether he was building a lighthouse or a first-class hotel. Browning knew perfectly well what he was doing; and if the reader does not like his art, at least the author did. The general sentiment expressed in the statement that he did not care about form is simply the most ridiculous criticism that could be conceived. It would be far nearer the truth to say that he cared more for form than any other English poet who ever lived. He was always weaving and modelling and inventing new forms. Among all his two hundred to three hundred poems it would scarcely be an exaggeration to say that there are half as many different metres as there are different poems.

The great English poets who are supposed to have cared more for form than Browning did, cared less at least in this sense—that they were content to use old forms so long as they were certain that they had new ideas. Browning, on the other hand, no sooner had a new idea than he tried to make a new form to express it. Wordsworth and Shelley were really original poets; their attitude of thought and feeling marked without doubt certain great changes in literature and philosophy. Nevertheless, the "Ode on the Intimations of Immortality" is a perfectly normal and traditional ode, and "Prometheus Unbound" is a perfectly genuine and traditional Greek lyrical drama. But if we study Browning honestly, nothing will strike us more than that he really created a large number of quite novel and quite admirable artistic forms. It is too often forgotten what and how excellent these were. *The Ring and the Book*, for example, is an illuminating departure in literary method—the method of telling the same story several times and trusting to the variety of human character to turn it into several different and equally interesting stories. *Pippa Passes*, to take another example, is a new and most fruitful form, a series of detached dramas connected only by the presence of one fugitive and isolated figure. The invention of these things is not merely like the writing of a good poem—it is something like the invention of the sonnet or the Gothic arch. The poet who makes them does not merely create himself—he creates other poets. It is so in a degree long past enumeration with regard to Browning's smaller poems. Such a pious and horrible lyric as "The Heretic's Tragedy," for instance, is absolutely original, with its weird and almost blood-curdling echo verses, mocking echoes indeed—

"And clipt of his wings in Paris square,
 They bring him now to be burned alive.

 [*And wanteth there grace of lute or clavicithern,
   ye shall say to confirm him who singeth*—

 We bring John now to be burned alive."

A hundred instances might, of course, be given. Milton's "Sonnet on his Blindness," or Keats's "Ode on a Grecian Urn," are both thoroughly original, but still we can point to other such sonnets and other such odes. But can any one mention any poem of exactly the same structural and literary type as "Fears and Scruples," as "The Householder," as "House" or "Shop," as "Nationality in Drinks," as "Sibrandus Schafnaburgensis," as "My Star," as "A Portrait," as any of "Ferishtah's Fancies," as any of the "Bad Dreams."

The thing which ought to be said about Browning by those who do not enjoy him is simply that they do not like his form; that they have studied the form, and think it a bad form. If more people said things of this sort, the world of criticism would gain almost unspeakably in clarity and common honesty. Browning put himself before the world as a good poet. Let those who think he failed call him a bad poet, and there will be an end of the matter. There are many styles in art which perfectly competent æsthetic judges cannot endure. For instance, it would be perfectly legitimate for a strict lover of Gothic to say that one of the monstrous rococo altar-pieces in the Belgian churches with bulbous clouds and oaken sun-rays seven feet long, was, in his opinion, ugly. But surely it would be perfectly ridiculous for any one to say that it had no form. A man's actual feelings about it might be better expressed by saying that it had too much. To say that Browning was merely a thinker because you think "Caliban upon Setebos" ugly, is precisely as absurd as it would be to call the author of the old Belgian altar-piece a man devoted only to the abstractions of religion. The truth about Browning is not that he was indifferent to technical beauty, but that he invented a particular kind of technical beauty to which any one else is free to be as indifferent as he chooses.

There is in this matter an extraordinary tendency to vague and unmeaning criticism. The usual way of criticising an author, particularly an author who has added something to the literary forms of the world, is to complain that his work does not contain something which is obviously the speciality of somebody else. The correct thing to say about Maeterlinck is that some play of his in which, let us say, a princess dies in a deserted tower by the sea, has a certain beauty, but that we look in vain in it for that robust geniality, that really boisterous will to live which may be found in *Martin Chuzzlewit*. The right thing to say about *Cyrano de Bergerac* is that it may have a certain kind of wit and spirit, but that it really throws no light on the duty of middle-aged married couples in Norway. It cannot be too much insisted upon that at least three-quarters of the blame and criticism commonly directed against artists and authors falls under this general objection, and is essentially valueless. Authors both great and small are, like everything else in existence, upon the whole greatly under-rated. They are blamed for not doing, not only what they have failed to do to reach their own ideal, but what they have never tried to do to reach every other writer's ideal. If we can show that Browning had a definite ideal of beauty and loyally pursued it, it is not necessary to prove that he could have written *In Memoriam* if he had tried.

Browning has suffered far more injustice from his admirers than from his opponents, for his admirers have for the most part got hold of the matter, so to speak, by the wrong end. They believe that what is ordinarily called the grotesque style of Browning was a kind of necessity boldly adopted by a great genius in order to express novel and profound ideas. But this is an entire mistake. What is called ugliness was to

Browning not in the least a necessary evil, but a quite unnecessary luxury, which he enjoyed for its own sake. For reasons that we shall see presently in discussing the philosophical use of the grotesque, it did so happen that Browning's grotesque style was very suitable for the expression of his peculiar moral and metaphysical view. But the whole mass of poems will be misunderstood if we do not realise first of all that he had a love of the grotesque of the nature of art for art's sake. Here, for example, is a short distinct poem merely descriptive of one of those elfish German jugs in which it is to be presumed Tokay had been served to him. This is the whole poem, and a very good poem too—

> "Up jumped Tokay on our table,
> Like a pigmy castle-warder,
> Dwarfish to see, but stout and able,
> Arms and accoutrements all in order;
> And fierce he looked North, then, wheeling South
> Blew with his bugle a challenge to Drouth,
> Cocked his flap-hat with the tosspot-feather,
> Twisted his thumb in his red moustache,
> Jingled his huge brass spurs together,
> Tightened his waist with its Buda sash,
> And then, with an impudence nought could abash,
> Shrugged his hump-shoulder, to tell the beholder,
> For twenty such knaves he would laugh but the bolder:
> And so, with his sword-hilt gallantly jutting,
> And dexter-hand on his haunch abutting,
> Went the little man, Sir Ausbruch, strutting!"

I suppose there are Browning students in existence who would think that this poem contained something pregnant about the Temperance question, or was a marvellously subtle analysis of the romantic movement in Germany. But surely to most of us it is sufficiently apparent that Browning was simply fashioning a ridiculous knick-knack, exactly as if he were actually moulding one of these preposterous German jugs. Now before studying the real character of this Browningesque style, there is one general truth to be recognised about Browning's work. It is this—that it is absolutely necessary to remember that Browning had, like every other poet, his simple and indisputable failures, and that it is one thing to speak of the badness of his artistic failures, and quite another thing to speak of the badness of his artistic aim. Browning's style may be a good style, and yet exhibit many examples of a thoroughly bad use of it. On this point there is indeed a singularly unfair system of judgment used by the public towards the poets. It is very little realised that the vast majority of great poets have written an enormous amount of very bad poetry. The unfortunate Wordsworth is generally supposed to be almost alone in this; but any one who thinks so can scarcely have read a certain number of the minor poems of Byron and Shelley and Tennyson.

Now it is only just to Browning that his more uncouth effusions should not be treated as masterpieces by which he must stand or fall, but treated simply as his failures. It is really true that such a line as

"Irks care the crop-full bird? Frets doubt the maw-crammed beast?"

is a very ugly and a very bad line. But it is quite equally true that Tennyson's

"And that good man, the clergyman, has told me words of peace,"

is a very ugly and a very bad line. But people do not

say that this proves that Tennyson was a mere crabbed controversialist and metaphysician. They say that it is a bad example of Tennyson's form; they do not say that it is a good example of Tennyson's indifference to form. Upon the whole, Browning exhibits far fewer instances of this failure in his own style than any other of the great poets, with the exception of one or two like Spenser and Keats, who seem to have a mysterious incapacity for writing bad poetry. But almost all original poets, particularly poets who have invented an artistic style, are subject to one most disastrous habit—the habit of writing imitations of themselves. Every now and then in the works of the noblest classical poets you will come upon passages which read like extracts from an American book of parodies. Swinburne, for example, when he wrote the couplet—

"From the lilies and languors of virtue
To the raptures and roses of vice,"

wrote what is nothing but a bad imitation of himself, an imitation which seems indeed to have the wholly unjust and uncritical object of proving that the Swinburnian melody is a mechanical scheme of initial letters. Or again, Mr. Rudyard Kipling when he wrote the line—

"Or ride with the reckless seraphim on the rim of a red-maned star,"

was caricaturing himself in the harshest and least sympathetic spirit of American humour. This tendency is, of course, the result of the self-consciousness and theatricality of modern life in which each of us is forced to conceive ourselves as part of a *dramatis personæ* and act perpetually in character. Browning sometimes yielded to this temptation to be a great deal too like himself.

> "Will I widen thee out till thou turnest
> From Margaret Minnikin mou' by God's grace,
> To Muckle-mouth Meg in good earnest."

This sort of thing is not to be defended in Browning any more than in Swinburne. But, on the other hand, it is not to be attributed in Swinburne to a momentary exaggeration, and in Browning to a vital æsthetic deficiency. In the case of Swinburne, we all feel that the question is not whether that particular preposterous couplet about lilies and roses redounds to the credit of the Swinburnian style, but whether it would be possible in any other style than the Swinburnian to have written the Hymn to Proserpine. In the same way, the essential issue about Browning as an artist is not whether he, in common with Byron, Wordsworth, Shelley, Tennyson, and Swinburne, sometimes wrote bad poetry, but whether in any other style except Browning's you could have achieved the precise artistic effect which is achieved by such incomparable lyrics as "The Patriot" or "The Laboratory." The answer must be in the negative, and in that answer lies the whole justification of Browning as an artist.

The question now arises, therefore, what was his conception of his functions as an artist? We have already agreed that his artistic originality concerned itself chiefly with the serious use of the grotesque. It becomes necessary, therefore, to ask what is the serious use of the grotesque, and what relation does the grotesque bear to the eternal and fundamental elements in life?

One of the most curious things to notice about popular æsthetic criticism is the number of phrases it will be found to use which are intended to express an æsthetic failure, and which express merely an æsthetic variety. Thus, for instance, the traveller will often hear the advice from local lovers of the picturesque, "The scenery round such and such a place has no interest; it is quite flat." To disparage scenery as quite flat is, of course, like disparaging a swan as quite white, or an Italian sky as quite blue. Flatness is a sublime quality in certain landscapes, just as rockiness is a sublime quality in others. In the same way there are a great number of phrases commonly used in order to disparage such writers as Browning which do not in fact disparage, but merely describe them. One of the most distinguished of Browning's biographers and critics says of him, for example, "He has never meant to be rugged, but has become so in striving after strength." To say that Browning never tried to be rugged is to say that Edgar Allan Poe never tried to be gloomy, or that Mr. W. S. Gilbert never tried to be extravagant. The whole issue depends upon whether we realise the simple and essential fact that ruggedness is a mode of art like gloominess or extravagance. Some poems ought to be rugged, just as some poems ought to be smooth. When we see a drift of stormy and fantastic clouds at sunset, we do not say that the cloud is beautiful although it is ragged at the edges. When we see a gnarled and sprawling oak, we do not say that it is fine although it is twisted. When we see a mountain, we do not say that it is impressive although it is rugged, nor do we say apologetically that it never meant to be rugged, but became so in its striving after strength. Now, to say that Browning's poems, artistically considered, are fine although they are rugged, is quite as absurd as to say that a rock, artistically considered, is fine although it is rugged. Ruggedness being an essential quality in the universe, there is that in man which responds to it as to the striking of any other chord of the eternal harmonies. As the children of nature, we are akin not only to the stars and flowers, but also to the toad-stools and the monstrous tropical birds. And it is to be repeated as the essential of the question that on this side of our nature we do emphatically love the form of the toad-stools, and not merely some complicated botanical and moral lessons which the philosopher may draw from them. For example, just as there is such a thing as a poetical metre being beautifully light or beautifully grave and haunting, so there is such a thing as a poetical metre being beautifully rugged. In the old ballads, for instance, every person of literary taste will be struck by a certain attractiveness in the bold, varying, irregular verse—

> "He is either himself a devil frae hell,
>   Or else his mother a witch maun be;
> I wadna have ridden that wan water
>   For a' the gowd in Christentie,"

is quite as pleasing to the ear in its own way as

> "There's a bower of roses by Bendemeer stream,
>   And the nightingale sings in it all the night long,"

is in another way. Browning had an unrivalled ear for this particular kind of staccato music. The absurd notion that he had no sense of melody in verse is only possible to people who think that there is no melody in

verse which is not an imitation of Swinburne. To give
a satisfactory idea of Browning's rhythmic originality
would be impossible without quotations more copious
than entertaining. But the essential point has been
suggested.

> "They were purple of raiment and golden,
>   Filled full of thee, fiery with wine,
> Thy lovers in haunts unbeholden,
>   In marvellous chambers of thine,"

is beautiful language, but not the only sort of beautiful
language. This, for instance, has also a tune in it—

> "I—'next poet.' No, my hearties,
>   I nor am, nor fain would be!
> Choose your chiefs and pick your parties,
>   Not one soul revolt to me!
> *   *   *   *
> Which of you did I enable
>   Once to slip inside my breast,
> There to catalogue and label
>   What I like least, what love best,
> Hope and fear, believe and doubt of,
>   Seek and shun, respect, deride,
> Who has right to make a rout of
>   Rarities he found inside?"

This quick, gallantly stepping measure also has its
own kind of music, and the man who cannot feel it can
never have enjoyed the sound of soldiers marching by.
This, then, roughly is the main fact to remember about
Browning's poetical method, or about any one's poetical
method—that the question is not whether that method
is the best in the world, but the question whether there
are not certain things which can only be conveyed by

that method. It is perfectly true, for instance, that a really lofty and lucid line of Tennyson, such as—

> "Thou art the highest, and most human too"

and

> "We needs must love the highest when we see it"

would really be made the worse for being translated into Browning. It would probably become

> "High's human; man loves best, best visible,"

and would lose its peculiar clarity and dignity and courtly plainness. But it is quite equally true that any really characteristic fragment of Browning, if it were only the tempestuous scolding of the organist in "Master Hugues of Saxe-Gotha"—

> "Hallo, you sacristan, show us a light there!
>   Down it dips, gone like a rocket.
> What, you want, do you, to come unawares,
> Sweeping the church up for first morning-prayers,
> And find a poor devil has ended his cares
> At the foot of your rotten-runged rat-riddled stairs?
>   Do I carry the moon in my pocket?"

—it is quite equally true that this outrageous gallop of rhymes ending with a frantic astronomical image would lose in energy and spirit if it were written in a conventional and classical style, and ran—

> "What must I deem then that thou dreamest to find
>   Disjected bones adrift upon the stair
> Thou sweepest clean, or that thou deemest that I
>   Pouch in my wallet the vice-regal sun?"

Is it not obvious that this statelier version might be excellent poetry of its kind, and yet would be bad exactly in so far as it was good; that it would lose all the swing, the rush, the energy of the preposterous and grotesque original? In fact, we may see how unmanageable is this classical treatment of the essentially absurd in Tennyson himself. The humorous passages in *The Princess*, though often really humorous in themselves, always appear forced and feeble because they have to be restrained by a certain metrical dignity, and the mere idea of such restraint is incompatible with humour. If Browning had written the passage which opens *The Princess*, descriptive of the "larking" of the villagers in the magnate's park, he would have spared us nothing; he would not have spared us the shrill uneducated voices and the unburied bottles of ginger beer. He would have crammed the poem with uncouth similes; he would have changed the metre a hundred times; he would have broken into doggerel and into rhapsody; but he would have left, when all is said and done, as he leaves in that paltry fragment of the grumbling organist, the impression of a certain eternal human energy. Energy and joy, the father and the mother of the grotesque, would have ruled the poem. We should have felt of that rowdy gathering little but the sensation of which Mr. Henley writes—

> "Praise the generous gods for giving,
> In this world of sin and strife,
> With some little time for living,
> Unto each the joy of life,"

the thought that every wise man has when looking at a Bank Holiday crowd at Margate.

To ask why Browning enjoyed this perverse and fantastic style most would be to go very deep into his spirit indeed, probably a great deal deeper than it is possible to go. But it is worth while to suggest tentatively the general function of the grotesque in art generally and in his art in particular. There is one very curious idea into which we have been hypnotised by the more eloquent poets, and that is that nature in the sense of what is ordinarily called the country is a thing entirely stately and beautiful as those terms are commonly understood. The whole world of the fantastic, all things top-heavy, lop sided, and nonsensical are conceived as the work of man, gargoyles, German jugs, Chinese pots, political caricatures, burlesque epics, the pictures of Mr. Aubrey Beardsley and the puns of Robert Browning. But in truth a part, and a very large part, of the sanity and power of nature lies in the fact that out of her comes all this instinct of caricature. Nature may present itself to the poet too often as consisting of stars and lilies; but these are not poets who live in the country; they are men who go to the country for inspiration and could no more live in the country than they could go to bed in Westminster Abbey. Men who live in the heart of nature, farmers and peasants, know that nature means cows and pigs, and creatures more humorous than can be found in a whole sketch-book of Callot. And the element of the grotesque in art, like the element of the grotesque in nature, means, in the main, energy, the energy which takes its own forms and goes its own way. Browning's verse, in so far as it is grotesque, is not complex or artificial; it is natural and in the legitimate tradition of nature. The verse sprawls like the trees, dances like the dust; it is ragged like the thunder-cloud, it is top-heavy like the toadstool.

Energy which disregards the standard of classical art is in nature as it is in Browning. The same sense of the uproarious force in things which makes Browning dwell on the oddity of a fungus or a jellyfish makes him dwell on the oddity of a philosophical idea. Here, for example, we have a random instance from "The Englishman in Italy" of the way in which Browning, when he was most Browning, regarded physical nature.

> "And pitch down his basket before us,
>   All trembling alive
> With pink and grey jellies, your sea-fruit;
>   You touch the strange lumps,
> And mouths gape there, eyes open, all manner
>   Of horns and of humps,
> Which only the fisher looks grave at."

Nature might mean flowers to Wordsworth and grass to Walt Whitman, but to Browning it really meant such things as these, the monstrosities and living mysteries of the sea. And just as these strange things meant to Browning energy in the physical world, so strange thoughts and strange images meant to him energy in the mental world. When, in one of his later poems, the professional mystic is seeking in a supreme moment of sincerity to explain that small things may be filled with God as well as great, he uses the very same kind of image, the image of a shapeless sea-beast, to embody that noble conception.

> "The Name comes close behind a stomach-cyst,
> The simplest of creations, just a sac
> That's mouth, heart, legs, and belly at once, yet lives
> And feels, and could do neither, we conclude,
> If simplified still further one degree."
>
>   (SLUDGE.)

These bulbous, indescribable sea-goblins are the first thing on which the eye of the poet lights in looking on a landscape, and the last in the significance of which he trusts in demonstrating the mercy of the Everlasting.

There is another and but slightly different use of the grotesque, but which is definitely valuable in Browning's poetry, and indeed in all poetry. To present a matter in a grotesque manner does certainly tend to touch the nerve of surprise and thus to draw attention to the intrinsically miraculous character of the object itself. It is difficult to give examples of the proper use of grotesqueness without becoming too grotesque. But we should all agree that if St. Paul's Cathedral were suddenly presented to us upside down we should, for the moment, be more surprised at it, and look at it more than we have done all the centuries during which it has rested on its foundations. Now it is the supreme function of the philosopher of the grotesque to make the world stand on its head that people may look at it. If we say "a man is a man" we awaken no sense of the fantastic, however much we ought to, but if we say, in the language of the old satirist, "that man is a two-legged bird, without feathers," the phrase does, for a moment, make us look at man from the outside and gives us a thrill in his presence. When the author of the Book of Job insists upon the huge, half-witted, apparently unmeaning magnificence and might of Behemoth, the hippopotamus, he is appealing precisely to this sense of wonder provoked by the grotesque. "Canst thou play with him as with a bird, canst thou bind him for thy maidens?" he says in an admirable passage. The notion of the hippopotamus as a household pet is curiously in the spirit of the humour of Browning.

But when it is clearly understood that Browning's love of the fantastic in style was a perfectly serious artistic love, when we understand that he enjoyed working in that style, as a Chinese potter might enjoy making dragons, or a mediæval mason making devils, there yet remains something definite which must be laid to his account as a fault. He certainly had a capacity for becoming perfectly childish in his indulgence in ingenuities that have nothing to do with poetry at all, such as puns, and rhymes, and grammatical structures that only just fit into each other like a Chinese puzzle. Probably it was only one of the marks of his singular vitality, curiosity, and interest in details. He was certainly one of those somewhat rare men who are fierily ambitious both in large things and in small. He prided himself on having written *The Ring and the Book*, and he also prided himself on knowing good wine when he tasted it. He prided himself on re-establishing optimism on a new foundation, and it is to be presumed, though it is somewhat difficult to imagine, that he prided himself on such rhymes as the following in *Pacchiarotto* :—

> "The wolf, fox, bear, and monkey,
>   By piping advice in one key—
> That his pipe should play a prelude
> To something heaven-tinged not hell-hued,
> Something not harsh but docile,
> Man-liquid, not man-fossil."

This writing, considered as writing, can only be regarded as a kind of joke, and most probably Browning considered it so himself. It has nothing at all to do with that powerful and symbolic use of the grotesque which may be found in such admirable passages as this from "Holy Cross Day":—

> "Give your first groan—compunction's at work;
> And soft! from a Jew you mount to a Turk.
> Lo, Micah—the self-same beard on chin
> He was four times already converted in!"

This is the serious use of the grotesque. Through it passion and philosophy are as well expressed as through any other medium. But the rhyming frenzy of Browning has no particular relation even to the poems in which it occurs. It is not a dance to any measure; it can only be called the horse-play of literature. It may be noted, for example, as a rather curious fact, that the ingenious rhymes are generally only mathematical triumphs, not triumphs of any kind of assonance. "The Pied Piper of Hamelin," a poem written for children, and bound in general to be lucid and readable, ends with a rhyme which it is physically impossible for any one to say:—

> "And, whether they pipe us free, fróm rats or fróm mice,
> If we've promised them aught, let us keep our promise!"

This queer trait in Browning, his inability to keep a kind of demented ingenuity even out of poems in which it was quite inappropriate, is a thing which must be recognised, and recognised all the more because as a whole he was a very perfect artist, and a particularly perfect artist in the use of the grotesque. But everywhere when we go a little below the surface in Browning we find that there was something in him perverse and unusual despite all his working normality and simplicity. His mind was perfectly wholesome, but it was not made exactly like the ordinary mind. It was like a piece of strong wood with a knot in it.

The quality of what can only be called buffoonery which is under discussion is indeed one of the many things in which Browning was more of an Elizabethan than a Victorian. He was like the Elizabethans in their belief in the normal man, in their gorgeous and over-loaded language, above all in their feeling for learning as an enjoyment and almost a frivolity. But there was nothing in which he was so thoroughly Elizabethan, and even Shakespearian, as in this fact, that when he felt inclined to write a page of quite uninteresting nonsense, he immediately did so. Many great writers have contrived to be tedious, and apparently aimless, while expounding some thought which they believed to be grave and profitable; but this frivolous stupidity had not been found in any great writer since the time of Rabelais and the time of the Elizabethans. In many of the comic scenes of Shakespeare we have precisely this elephantine ingenuity, this hunting of a pun to death through three pages. In the Elizabethan dramatists and in Browning it is no doubt to a certain extent the mark of a real hilarity. People must be very happy to be so easily amused.

In the case of what is called Browning's obscurity, the question is somewhat more difficult to handle. Many people have supposed Browning to be profound because he was obscure, and many other people, hardly less mistaken, have supposed him to be obscure because he was profound. He was frequently profound, he was occasionally obscure, but as a matter of fact the two have little or nothing to do with each other. Browning's dark and elliptical mode of speech, like his love of the grotesque, was simply a characteristic of his, a trick of his temperament, and had little or nothing to do with whether what he was expressing was profound or superficial. Suppose, for example, that a person well read in English poetry but unacquainted with Browning's style were earnestly invited to consider the following verse:—

> "Hobbs hints blue—straight he turtle eats.
> Nobbs prints blue—claret crowns his cup.
> Nokes outdares Stokes in azure feats—
> Both gorge. Who fished the murex up?
> What porridge had John Keats?"

The individual so confronted would say without hesitation that it must indeed be an abstruse and indescribable thought which could only be conveyed by remarks so completely disconnected. But the point of the matter is that the thought contained in this amazing verse is not abstruse or philosophical at all, but is a perfectly ordinary and straightforward comment, which any one might have made upon an obvious fact of life. The whole verse of course begins to explain itself, if we know the meaning of the word "murex," which is the name of a sea-shell, out of which was made the celebrated blue dye of Tyre. The poet takes this blue dye as a simile for a new fashion in literature, and points out that Hobbs, Nobbs, etc., obtain fame and comfort by merely using the dye from the shell; and adds the perfectly natural comment:—

> ". . . Who fished the murex up?
> What porridge had John Keats?"

So that the verse is not subtle, and was not meant to be subtle, but is a perfectly casual piece of sentiment at the end of a light poem. Browning is not obscure because he has such deep things to say, any more than he is grotesque because he has such new things to say. He is both of these things primarily, because he likes to express himself in a particular manner. The manner is as natural to him as a man's physical voice, and it is abrupt, sketchy, allusive, and full of gaps. Here comes in the fundamental difference between Browning and such a writer as George Meredith, with whom the Philistine satirist would so often in the matter of complexity class him. The works of George Meredith are, as it were, obscure even when we know what they mean. They deal with nameless emotions, fugitive sensations, subconscious certainties and uncertainties, and it really requires a somewhat curious and unfamiliar mode of speech to indicate the presence of these. But the great part of Browning's actual sentiments, and almost all the finest and most literary of them, are perfectly plain and popular and eternal sentiments. Meredith is really a singer producing strange notes and cadences difficult to follow because of the delicate rhythm of the song he sings. Browning is simply a great demagogue, with an impediment in his speech. Or rather, to speak more strictly, Browning is a man whose excitement for the glory of the obvious is so great that his speech becomes disjointed and precipitate: he becomes eccentric through his advocacy of the ordinary, and goes mad for the love of sanity.

If Browning and George Meredith were each describing the same act, they might both be obscure, but their obscurities would be entirely different. Suppose, for instance, they were describing even so prosaic and material an act as a man being knocked downstairs by another man to whom he had given the lie, Meredith's description would refer to something which an ordinary observer would not see, or at least could not describe. It might be a sudden sense of anarchy in the brain of the assaulter, or a stupefaction and stunned serenity in that of the object of the assault. He might write, "Wainwood's 'Men vary in veracity,' brought the baronet's arm up. He felt the doors of his brain burst, and Wainwood a swift rushing of himself through air accompanied with a clarity as of the annihilated." Meredith, in other words, would speak queerly because he was describing queer mental experiences. But Browning might simply be describing the material incident of the man being knocked downstairs, and his description would run:—

"What then? 'You lie' and doormat below stairs
 Takes bump from back."

This is not subtlety, but merely a kind of insane swiftness. Browning is not like Meredith, anxious to pause and examine the sensations of the combatants, nor does he become obscure through this anxiety. He is only so anxious to get his man to the bottom of the stairs quickly that he leaves out about half the story.

Many who could understand that ruggedness might be an artistic quality, would decisively, and in most cases rightly, deny that obscurity could under any conceivable circumstances be an artistic quality. But here again Browning's work requires a somewhat more cautious and sympathetic analysis. There is a certain kind of fascination, a strictly artistic fascination, which arises from a matter being hinted at in such a way as to leave a certain tormenting uncertainty even at the end. It is well sometimes to half understand a poem in the same manner that we half understand the world. One of the deepest and strangest of all human moods is the mood which will suddenly strike us perhaps in a garden at night, or deep in sloping meadows, the feeling that every flower and leaf has just uttered something stupendously direct and important, and that we have by a prodigy of imbecility not heard or understood it. There is a certain poetic value, and that a genuine one, in this sense of having missed the full meaning of things. There is beauty, not only in wisdom, but in this dazed and dramatic ignorance.

But in truth it is very difficult to keep pace with all the strange and unclassified artistic merits of Browning. He was always trying experiments; sometimes he failed, producing clumsy and irritating metres, top-heavy and over-concentrated thought. Far more often he triumphed, producing a crowd of boldly designed poems, every one of which taken separately might have founded an artistic school. But whether successful or unsuccessful, he never ceased from his fierce hunt after poetic novelty. He never became a conservative. The last book he published in his life-time, *Parleyings with Certain People of Importance in their Day*, was a new poem, and more revolutionary than *Paracelsus*. This is the true light in which to regard Browning as an artist. He had determined to leave no spot of the cosmos unadorned by his poetry which he could find it possible to adorn. An admirable example can be found in that splendid poem "Childe

Roland to the Dark Tower came." It is the hint of an entirely new and curious type of poetry, the poetry of the shabby and hungry aspect of the earth itself. Daring poets who wished to escape from conventional gardens and orchards had long been in the habit of celebrating the poetry of rugged and gloomy landscapes, but Browning is not content with this. He insists upon celebrating the poetry of mean landscapes. That sense of scrubbiness in nature, as of a man unshaved, had never been conveyed with this enthusiasm and primeval gusto before.

> "If there pushed any ragged thistle-stalk
>   Above its mates, the head was chopped; the bents
>   Were jealous else. What made those holes and rents
> In the dock's harsh swarth leaves, bruised as to baulk
> All hope of greenness? 'tis a brute must walk
>   Pashing their life out, with a brute's intents."

This is a perfect realisation of that eerie sentiment which comes upon us, not so often among mountains and water-falls, as it does on some half-starved common at twilight, or in walking down some grey mean street. It is the song of the beauty of refuse; and Browning was the first to sing it. Oddly enough it has been one of the poems about which most of those pedantic and trivial questions have been asked, which are asked invariably by those who treat Browning as a science instead of a poet, "What does the poem of 'Childe Roland' mean?" The only genuine answer to this is, "What does anything mean?" Does the earth mean nothing? Do grey skies and wastes covered with thistles mean nothing? Does an old horse turned out to graze mean nothing? If it does, there is but one further truth to be added—that everything means nothing.

CHAPTER VII

THE RING AND THE BOOK

WHEN we have once realised the great conception of the plan of *The Ring and the Book,* the studying of a single matter from nine different stand-points, it becomes exceedingly interesting to notice what these stand-points are; what figures Browning has selected as voicing the essential and distinct versions of the case. One of the ablest and most sympathetic of all the critics of Browning, Mr. Augustine Birrell, has said in one place that the speeches of the two advocates in *The Ring and the Book* will scarcely be very interesting to the ordinary reader. However that may be, there can be little doubt that a great number of the readers of Browning think them beside the mark and adventitious. But it is exceedingly dangerous to say that anything in Browning is irrelevant or unnecessary. We are apt to go on thinking so until some mere trifle puts the matter in a new light, and the detail that seemed meaningless springs up as almost the central pillar of the structure. In the successive monologues of his poem, Browning is endeavouring to depict the various strange ways in which a fact gets itself presented to the world. In every question there are partisans who bring cogent and convincing arguments for the right side; there are also partisans who bring cogent and convincing arguments for the wrong side. But over and above these, there does exist in every great controversy a class of more or less official partisans who are continually engaged in defending each cause by entirely inappropriate arguments. They do not know the real good that can be said for the good cause, nor the real good that can be said for the bad one. They are represented by the animated, learned, eloquent, ingenious, and entirely futile and impertinent arguments of Juris Doctor Bottinius and Dominus Hyacinthus de Archangelis. These two men brilliantly misrepresent, not merely each other's cause, but their own cause. The introduction of them is one of the finest and most artistic strokes in *The Ring and the Book*.

We can see the matter best by taking an imaginary parallel. Suppose that a poet of the type of Browning lived some centuries hence and found in some *cause célèbre* of our day, such as the Parnell Commission, an opportunity for a work similar in its design to *The Ring and the Book*. The first monologue, which would be called "Half-London," would be the arguments of an ordinary educated and sensible Unionist who believed that there really was evidence that the Nationalist movement in Ireland was rooted in crime and public panic. The "Other half-London" would be the utterance of an ordinary educated and sensible Home Ruler, who thought that in the main Nationalism was one distinct symptom, and crime another, of the same poisonous and stagnant problem. The "Tertium Quid" would be some detached intellectual, committed neither to Nationalism nor to Unionism, possibly Mr. Bernard Shaw, who would make a very entertaining Browning monologue. Then of course would come the speeches of the great actors in the drama, the icy anger of Parnell, the shuffling apologies of Pigott. But we should feel that the record was incomplete without another touch which in practice has so much to do with the confusion of such a question. Bottinius and Hyacinthus de Archangelis, the two cynical professional pleaders, with their transparent assumptions and incredible theories of the case, would be represented by two party journalists; one of whom was ready to base his case either on the fact that Parnell was a Socialist or an Anarchist, or an Atheist or a Roman Catholic; and the other of whom was ready to base his case on the theory that Lord Salisbury hated Parnell or was in league with him, or had never heard of him, or anything else that was remote from the world of reality. These are the kind of little touches for which we must always be on the look-out in Browning. Even if a digression, or a simile, or a whole scene in a play, seems to have no point or value, let us wait a little and give it a chance. He very seldom wrote anything that did not mean a great deal.

It is sometimes curious to notice how a critic, possessing no little cultivation and fertility, will, in speaking of a work of art, let fall almost accidentally some apparently trivial comment, which reveals to us with an instantaneous and complete mental illumination the fact that he does not, so far as that work of art is concerned, in the smallest degree understand what he is talking about. He may have intended to correct merely some minute detail of the work he is studying, but that single movement is enough to blow him and all his diplomas into the air. These are the sensations with which the true Browningite will regard the criticism made by so many of Browning's critics and biographers about *The Ring and the Book*. That criticism was embodied by one of them in the words "the theme looked at dispassionately is unworthy of the monument in which it is entombed for eternity." Now this remark shows at once that the critic does not know what *The Ring and the Book* means. We feel about it as we should feel about a man who said that the plot of *Tristram Shandy* was not well constructed, or that the women in Rossetti's pictures did not look useful and industrious. A man who has missed the fact that *Tristram Shandy* is a game of digressions, that the whole book is a kind of practical joke to cheat the reader out of a story, simply has not read *Tristram Shandy* at all. The man who objects to the Rossetti pictures because they depict a sad and sensuous day-dream, objects to their existing at all. And any one who objects to Browning writing his huge epic round a trumpery and sordid police-case has in reality missed the whole length and breadth of the poet's meaning. The essence of *The Ring and the Book* is that it is the great epic of the nineteenth century, because it is the great epic of the enormous importance of small things. The supreme difference that divides *The Ring and the Book* from all the great poems of similar length and largeness of design is precisely the fact that all these are about affairs commonly called important, and *The Ring and the Book* is about an affair commonly called contemptible. Homer says, "I will show you the relations between man and heaven as exhibited in a great legend of love and war, which shall contain the mightiest of all mortal warriors, and the most beautiful of all mortal women." The author of the Book of Job says, "I will show you the relations between man and heaven by a tale of primeval sorrows and the voice of God out of a whirlwind." Virgil says, "I will show you the relations of man to heaven by the tale of the origin of the greatest people and the founding of the most wonderful city in the world." Dante says, "I will show you the relations of man to heaven by uncovering the very machinery of the spiritual universe, and letting you hear, as I have heard, the roaring of the mills of God." Milton says, "I will show you the relations of man to heaven by telling you of the very beginning of all things, and the first shaping of the thing that is evil in the first twilight of time." Browning says, "I will show you the relations of man to heaven by telling you a story out of a dirty Italian book of criminal trials from which I select one of the meanest and most completely forgotten." Until we have realised this fundamental idea in *The Ring and the Book* all criticism is misleading.

In this Browning is, of course, the supreme embodiment of his time. The characteristic of the modern movements *par excellence* is the apotheosis of the insignificant. Whether it be the school of poetry which sees more in one cowslip or clover-top than in forests and waterfalls, or the school of fiction which finds something indescribably significant in the pattern of a hearth-rug, or the tint of a man's tweed coat, the tendency is the same. Maeterlinck stricken still and wondering by a deal door half open, or the light shining out of a window at night; Zola filling note-books with the medical significance of the twitching of a man's toes, or the loss of his appetite; Whitman counting the grass and the heart-shaped leaves of the lilac; Mr. George Gissing lingering fondly over the third-class ticket and the dilapidated umbrella; George Meredith seeing a soul's tragedy in a phrase at the dinner-table; Mr. Bernard Shaw filling three pages with stage directions to describe a parlour; all these men, different in every other particular, are alike in this, that they have ceased to believe certain things to be important and the rest to be unimportant. Significance is to them a wild thing that may leap upon them from any hiding-place. They have all become terribly impressed with and a little bit alarmed at the mysterious powers of small things. Their difference from the old epic poets is the whole difference between an age that fought with dragons and an age that fights with microbes.

This tide of the importance of small things is flowing so steadily around us upon every side to-day, that we do not sufficiently realise that if there was one man in English literary history who might with justice be called its fountain and origin, that man was Robert Browning. When Browning arose, literature was entirely in the hands of the Tennysonian poet. The Tennysonian poet does indeed mention trivialities, but he mentions them when he wishes to speak trivially; Browning mentions trivialities when he wishes to speak sensationally. Now this sense of the terrible importance of detail was a sense which may be said to have possessed Browning in the emphatic manner of a demoniac possession. Sane as he was, this one feeling might have driven him to a condition not far from madness. Any room that he was sitting in glared at him with innumerable eyes and mouths gaping with a story. There was sometimes no background and no middle distance in his mind. A human face and the pattern on the wall behind it came forward with equally aggressive clearness. It may be repeated, that if ever he who had the strongest head in the world had gone mad, it would have been through this turbulent democracy of things. If he looked at a porcelain vase or an old hat, a cabbage, or a puppy at play, each began to be bewitched with the spell of a kind of fairyland of philosophers: the vase, like the jar in the *Arabian Nights*, to send up a smoke of thoughts and shapes; the hat to produce souls, as a conjuror's hat produces rabbits; the cabbage to swell and overshadow the earth, like the Tree of Knowledge; and the puppy to go off at a scamper along the road to the end of the world. Any one who has read Browning's longer poems knows how constantly a simile or figure of speech is selected, not among the large, well-recognised figures common in poetry, but from some dusty corner of experience, and how often it is characterised by smallness and a certain quaint exactitude which could not have been found in any more usual example. Thus, for instance, *Prince Hohenstiel-Schwangau* explains the psychological meaning of all his restless and unscrupulous activities by comparing them to the impulse which has just led him, even in the act of talking, to draw a black line on the blotting-paper exactly, so as to connect two separate blots that were already there. This queer example is selected as the best possible instance of a certain fundamental restlessness and desire to add a touch to things in the spirit of man. I have no doubt whatever that Browning thought of the idea after doing the thing himself, and sat in a philosophical trance staring at a piece of inked blotting-paper, conscious that at that moment, and in that insignificant act, some immemorial monster of the mind, nameless from the beginning of the world, had risen to the surface of the spiritual sea.

It is therefore the very essence of Browning's genius, and the very essence of *The Ring and the Book*, that it should be the enormous multiplication of a small theme. It is the extreme of idle criticism to complain that the story is a current and sordid story, for the whole object of the poem is to show what infinities of spiritual good and evil a current and sordid story may contain. When once this is realised, it explains at one stroke the innumerable facts about the work. It explains, for example, Browning's detailed and picturesque account of the glorious dust-bin of odds and ends for sale, out of which he picked the printed record of the trial, and his insistence on its cheapness, its dustiness, its yellow leaves, and its crabbed Latin. The more soiled and dark and insignificant he can make the text appear, the better for his ample and gigantic sermon. It explains again the strictness with which Browning adhered to the facts of the forgotten intrigue. He was playing the game of seeing how much was really involved in one paltry fragment of fact. To have introduced large quantities of fiction would not have been sportsmanlike. *The Ring and the Book* therefore, to re-capitulate the view arrived at so far, is the typical epic of our age, because it expresses the richness of life by taking as a text a poor story. It pays to existence the highest of all possible compliments—the great compliment which monarchy paid to mankind—the compliment of selecting from it almost at random.

But this is only the first half of the claim of *The Ring and the Book* to be the typical epic of modern times. The second half of that claim, the second respect in which the work is representative of all modern development, requires somewhat more careful statement. *The Ring and the Book* is of course, essentially speaking, a detective story. Its difference from the ordinary detective story is that it seeks to establish, not the centre of criminal guilt, but the centre of spiritual guilt. But it has exactly the same kind of exciting quality that a detective story has, and a very excellent quality it is. But the element which is important, and which now requires pointing out, is the method by which that centre of spiritual guilt and the corresponding centre of spiritual rectitude is discovered. In order to make clear the peculiar character of this method, it is necessary to begin rather nearer the beginning, and to go back some little way in literary history.

I do not know whether anybody, including the editor himself, has ever noticed a peculiar coincidence which may be found in the arrangement of the lyrics in Sir Francis Palgrave's *Golden Treasury*. However that may be, two poems, each of them extremely well known, are placed side by side, and their juxtaposition represents one vast revolution in the poetical manner of looking at things. The first is Goldsmith's almost too well known.

> "When lovely woman stoops to folly,
>   And finds too late that men betray,
> What charm can soothe her melancholy?
>   What art can wash her guilt away?"

Immediately afterwards comes, with a sudden and thrilling change of note, the voice of Burns:—

> "Ye banks and braes o' bonnie Doon,
>   How can ye bloom sae fair?
> How can ye chant, ye little birds,
>   And I sae fu' of care?
>
> Thou'll break my heart, thou bonny bird,
>   That sings upon the bough,
> Thou minds me of the happy days
>   When my fause Love was true."

A man might read those two poems a great many times without happening to realise that they are two poems on exactly the same subject—the subject of a trusting woman deserted by a man. And the whole difference—the difference struck by the very first note of the voice of any one who reads them—is this fundamental difference, that Goldsmith's words are spoken about a certain situation, and Burns's words are spoken in that situation.

In the transition from one of these lyrics to the other, we have a vital change in the conception of the functions of the poet; a change of which Burns was in many ways the beginning, of which Browning, in a manner that we shall see presently, was the culmination.

Goldsmith writes fully and accurately in the tradition of the old historic idea of what a poet was. The poet, the *vates*, was the supreme and absolute critic of human existence, the chorus in the human drama; he was, to employ two words, which when analysed are the same word, either a spectator or a seer. He took a situation, such as the situation of a woman deserted by a man before-mentioned, and he gave, as Goldsmith gives, his own personal and definite decision upon it, entirely based upon general principles, and entirely from the outside. Then, as in the case of *The Golden Treasury*, he has no sooner given judgment than there comes a bitter and confounding cry out of the very heart of the situation itself, which tells us things which would have been quite left out of account by the poet of the general rule. No one, for example, but a person who knew something of the inside of agony would have introduced that touch of the rage of the mourner against the chattering frivolity of nature, "Thou'll break my heart, thou bonny bird." We find and could find no such touch in Goldsmith. We have to arrive at the conclusion therefore, that the *vates* or poet in his absolute capacity is defied and overthrown by this new method of what may be called the songs of experience.

Now Browning, as he appears in *The Ring and the Book*, represents the attempt to discover, not the truth in the sense that Goldsmith states it, but the larger truth which is made up of all the emotional experiences, such as that rendered by Burns. Browning, like Goldsmith, seeks ultimately to be just and impartial, but he does it by endeavouring to feel acutely every kind of partiality. Goldsmith stands apart from all the passions of the case, and Browning includes them all. If Browning were endeavouring to do strict justice in a case like that of the deserted lady by the banks of Doon, he would not touch or modify in the smallest particular the song as Burns sang it, but he would write other songs, perhaps equally pathetic. A lyric or a soliloquy would convince us suddenly by the mere pulse of its language, that there was some pathos in the other actors in the drama; some pathos, for example, in a weak man, conscious that in a passionate ignorance of life he had thrown away his power of love, lacking the moral courage to throw his prospects after it. We should be reminded again that there was some pathos in the position, let us say, of the seducer's mother, who had built all her hopes upon developments which a mésalliance would overthrow, or in the position of some rival lover, stricken to the ground with the tragedy in which he had not even the miserable comfort of a *locus standi*. All these characters in the story, Browning would realise from their own emotional point of view before he gave judgment. The poet in his ancient office held a kind of terrestrial day of judgment, and gave men halters and haloes; Browning gives men neither halter nor halo, he gives them voices. This is indeed the most bountiful of all the functions of the poet, that he gives men words, for which men from the beginning of the world have starved more than for bread.

Here then we have the second great respect in which *The Ring and the Book* is the great epic of the age. It is the great epic of the age, because it is the expression of the belief, it might almost be said, of the discovery, that no man ever lived upon this earth without possessing a point of view. No one ever lived who had not a little more to say for himself than any formal system of justice was likely to say for him. It is scarcely necessary to point out how entirely the application of this principle would revolutionise the old heroic epic, in which the poet decided absolutely the moral relations and moral value of the characters. Suppose, for example, that Homer had written the *Odyssey* on the principle of *The Ring and the Book*, how disturbing, how weird an experience it would be to read the story from the point of view of Antinous! Without contradicting a single material fact, without telling a single deliberate lie, the narrative would so change the whole world around us, that we should scarcely know we were dealing with the same place and people. The calm face of Penelope would, it may be, begin to grow meaner before our eyes, like a face changing in a dream. She would begin to appear as a fickle and selfish woman, passing falsely as a widow, and playing a double game between the attentions of foolish but honourable young men, and the fitful appearances of a wandering and good-for-nothing sailor-husband; a man prepared to act that most well-worn of melodramatic rôles, the conjugal bully and blackmailer, the man who uses marital rights as an instrument for the worse kind of wrongs. Or, again, if we had the story of the fall of King Arthur told from the stand-point of Mordred, it would only be a matter of a word or two; in a turn, in the twinkling of an eye, we should find ourselves sympathising with the efforts of an earnest young man to frustrate the profligacies of high-placed paladins like Lancelot and Tristram, and ultimately discovering, with deep regret but unshaken moral courage, that there was no way to frustrate them, except by overthrowing the cold and priggish and incapable egotist who ruled the country, and the whole artificial and bombastic schemes which bred these moral evils. It might be that in spite of this new view of the case, it would ultimately appear that Ulysses was really right and Arthur was really right, just as Browning makes it ultimately appear that Pompilia was really right. But any one can see the enormous difference in scope and difficulty between the old epic which told the whole story from one man's point of view, and the new epic which cannot come to its conclusion, until it has digested and assimilated views as paradoxical and disturbing as our imaginary defence of Antinous and apologia of Mordred.

One of the most important steps ever taken in the history of the world is this step, with all its various aspects, literary, political, and social, which is represented by *The Ring and the Book*. It is the step of deciding, in the face of many serious dangers and disadvantages, to let everybody talk. The poet of the old epic is the poet who had learnt to speak; Browning in the new epic is the poet who has learnt to listen. This listening to truth and error, to heretics, to fools, to intellectual bullies, to desperate partisans, to mere chatterers, to systematic poisoners of the mind, is the hardest lesson that humanity has ever been set to learn. *The Ring and the Book* is the embodiment of this terrible magnanimity and patience. It is the epic of free speech.

Free speech is an idea which has at present all the unpopularity of a truism; so that we tend to forget that it was not so very long ago that it had the more practical unpopularity which attaches to a new truth. Ingratitude is surely the chief of the intellectual sins of man. He takes his political benefits for granted, just as he takes the skies and the seasons for granted. He considers the calm of a city street a thing as inevitable as the calm of a forest clearing, whereas it is only kept in peace by a sustained stretch and effort similar to that which keeps up a battle or a fencing match. Just as we forget where we stand in relation to natural phenomena, so we forget it in relation to social phenomena. We forget that the earth is a star, and we forget that free speech is a paradox.

It is not by any means self-evident upon the face of it that an institution like the liberty of speech is right or just. It is not natural or obvious to let a man utter follies and abominations which you believe to be bad for mankind any more than it is natural or obvious to let a man dig up a part of the public road, or infect half a town with typhoid fever. The theory of free speech, that truth is so much larger and stranger and more many-sided than we know of, that it is very much better at all costs to hear every one's account of it, is a theory which has been justified upon the whole by experiment, but which remains a very daring and even a very surprising theory. It is really one of the great discoveries of the modern time; but, once admitted, it is a principle that does not merely affect politics, but philosophy, ethics, and finally poetry.

Browning was upon the whole the first poet to apply the principle to poetry. He perceived that if we wish to tell the truth about a human drama, we must not tell it merely like a melodrama, in which the villain is villainous and the comic man is comic. He saw that the truth had not been told until he had seen in the villain the pure and disinterested gentleman that most villains firmly believe themselves to be, or until he had taken the comic man as seriously as it is the custom of comic men to take themselves. And in this Browning is beyond all question the founder of the most modern school of poetry. Everything that was profound, everything, indeed, that was tolerable in the æsthetes of 1880, and the decadent of 1890, has its ultimate source in Browning's great conception that every one's point of view is interesting, even if it be a jaundiced or a blood-shot point of view. He is at one with the decadents, in holding that it is emphatically profitable, that it is emphatically creditable, to know something of the grounds of the happiness of a thoroughly bad man. Since his time we have indeed been somewhat over-satisfied with the moods of the burglar, and the pensive lyrics of the receiver of stolen goods. But Browning, united with the decadents on this point, of the value of every human testimony, is divided from them sharply and by a chasm in another equally important point. He held that it is necessary to listen to all sides of a question in order to discover the truth of it. But he held that there was a truth to discover. He held that justice was a mystery, but not, like the decadents, that justice was a delusion. He held, in other words, the true Browning doctrine, that in a dispute every one was to a certain extent right; not the decadent doctrine that in so mad a place as the world, every one must be by the nature of things wrong.

Browning's conception of the Universe can hardly be better expressed than in the old and pregnant fable about the five blind men who went to visit an elephant.

One of them seized its trunk, and asserted that an elephant was a kind of serpent; another embraced its leg, and was ready to die for the belief that an elephant was a kind of tree. In the same way to the man who leaned against its side it was a wall; to the man who had hold of its tail a rope, and to the man who ran upon its tusk a particularly unpleasant kind of spear. This, as I have said, is the whole theology and philosophy of Browning. But he differs from the psychological decadents and impressionists in this important point, that he thinks that although the blind men found out very little about the elephant, the elephant was an elephant, and was there all the time. The blind men formed mistaken theories because an elephant is a thing with a very curious shape. And Browning firmly believed that the Universe was a thing with a very curious shape indeed. No blind poet could even imagine an elephant without experience, and no man, however great and wise, could dream of God and not die. But there is a vital distinction between the mystical view of Browning, that the blind men are misled because there is so much for them to learn, and the purely impressionist and agnostic view of the modern poet, that the blind men were misled because there was nothing for them to learn. To the impressionist artist of our time we are not blind men groping after an elephant and naming it a tree or a serpent. We are maniacs, isolated in separate cells, and dreaming of trees and serpents without reason and without result.

CHAPTER VIII

THE PHILOSOPHY OF BROWNING

THE great fault of most of the appreciation of Browning lies in the fact that it conceives the moral and artistic value of his work to lie in what is called "the message of Browning," or "the teaching of Browning," or, in other words, in the mere opinions of Browning. Now Browning had opinions, just as he had a dress-suit or a vote for Parliament. He did not hesitate to express these opinions any more than he would have hesitated to fire off a gun, or open an umbrella, if he had possessed those articles, and realised their value. For example, he had, as his students and eulogists have constantly stated, certain definite opinions about the spiritual function of love, or the intellectual basis of Christianity. Those opinions were very striking and very solid, as everything was which came out of Browning's mind. His two great theories of the universe may be expressed in two comparatively parallel phrases. The first was what may be called the hope which lies in the imperfection of man. The characteristic poem of "Old Pictures in Florence" expresses very quaintly and beautifully the idea that some hope may always be based on deficiency itself; in other words, that in so far as man is a one-legged or a one-eyed creature, there is something about his appearance which indicates that he should have another leg and another eye The poem suggests admirably that such a sense of incompleteness may easily be a great advance upon a sense of completeness, that the part may easily and obviously be greater than the whole. And from this Browning draws, as he is fully justified in drawing, a definite hope for immortality and the larger scale of life. For nothing is more certain than that though this world is the only world that we have known, or of which we could even dream, the fact does remain that we have named it "a strange world." In other words, we have certainly felt that this world did not explain itself, that something in its complete and patent picture has been omitted. And Browning was right in saying that in a cosmos where incompleteness implies completeness, life implies immortality. This then was the first of the doctrines or opinions of Browning: the hope that lies in the imperfection of man. The second of the great Browning doctrines requires some audacity to express. It can only be properly stated as the hope that lies in the imperfection of God. That is to say, that Browning held that sorrow and self-denial, if they were the burdens of man, were also his privileges. He held that these stubborn sorrows and obscure valours might, to use a yet more strange expression, have provoked the envy of the Almighty. If man has self-sacrifice and God has none, then man has in the Universe a secret and blasphemous superiority. And this tremendous story of a Divine jealousy Browning reads into the story of the Crucifixion. If the Creator had not been crucified He would not have been as great as thousands of wretched fanatics among His own creatures. It is needless to insist upon this point; any one who wishes to read it splendidly expressed need only be referred to "Saul." But these are emphatically the two main doctrines or opinions of Browning which I have ventured to characterise roughly as the hope in the imperfection of man, and more boldly as the hope in the imperfection of God. They are great thoughts, thoughts written by a great man, and they raise noble and beautiful doubts on behalf of faith which the human spirit will never answer or exhaust. But about them in connection with Browning there nevertheless remains something to be added.

Browning was, as most of his upholders and all his opponents say, an optimist. His theory, that man's sense of his own imperfection implies a design of perfection, is a very good argument for optimism. His theory that man's knowledge of and desire for self-sacrifice implies God's knowledge of and desire for self-sacrifice is another very good argument for optimism. But any one will make the deepest and blackest and most incurable mistake about Browning who imagines that his optimism was founded on any arguments for optimism. Because he had a strong intellect, because he had a strong power of conviction, he conceived and developed and asserted these doctrines of the incompleteness of Man and the sacrifice of Omnipotence. But these doctrines were the symptoms of his optimism, they were not its origin. It is surely obvious that no one can be argued into optimism since no one can be argued into happiness. Browning's optimism was not founded on opinions which were the work of Browning, but on life which was the work of God. One of Browning's most celebrated biographers has said that something of Browning's theology must be put down to his possession of a good digestion. The remark was, of course, like all remarks touching the tragic subject of digestion, intended to be funny and to convey some kind of doubt or diminution touching the value of Browning's faith. But if we examine the matter with somewhat greater care we shall see that it is indeed a thorough compliment to that faith. Nobody, strictly speaking, is happier on account of his digestion. He is happy because he is so constituted as to forget all about it. Nobody really is convulsed with delight at the thought of the ingenious machinery which he possesses inside him; the thing which delights him is simply the full possession of his own human body. I cannot in the least understand why a good digestion—that is, a good body—should not be held to be as mystic a benefit as a sunset or the first flower of spring. But there is about digestion this peculiarity throwing a great light on human pessimism, that it is one of the many things which we never speak of as existing until they go wrong. We should think it ridiculous to speak of a man as suffering from his boots if we meant that he had really no boots. But we do speak of a man suffering from digestion when we mean that he suffers from a lack of digestion. In the same way we speak of a man suffering from nerves when we mean that his nerves are more inefficient than any one else's nerves. If any one wishes to see how grossly language can degenerate, he need only compare the old optimistic use of the word nervous, which we employ in speaking of a nervous grip, with the new pessimistic use of the word, which we employ in speaking of a nervous manner. And as digestion is a good thing which sometimes goes wrong, as nerves are good things which sometimes go wrong, so existence itself in the eyes of Browning and all the great optimists is a good thing which sometimes goes wrong. He held himself as free to draw his inspiration from the gift of good health as from the gift of learning or the gift of fellowship. But he held that such gifts were in life innumerable and varied, and that every man, or at least almost every man, possessed some window looking out on this essential excellence of things.

Browning's optimism then, since we must continue to use this somewhat inadequate word, was a result of experience—experience which is for some mysterious reason generally understood in the sense of sad or disillusioning experience. An old gentleman rebuking a little boy for eating apples in a tree is in the common conception the type of experience. If he really wished to be a type of experience he would climb up the tree himself and proceed to experience the apples. Browning's faith was founded upon joyful experience, not in the sense that he selected his joyful experiences and ignored his painful ones, but in the sense that his joyful experiences selected themselves and stood out in his memory by virtue of their own extraordinary intensity of colour. He did not use experience in that mean and pompous sense in which it is used by the worldling advanced in years. He rather used it in that healthier and more joyful sense in which it is used at revivalist meetings. In the

Salvation Army a man's experiences mean his experiences of the mercy of God, and to Browning the meaning was much the same. But the revivalists' confessions deal mostly with experiences of prayer and praise; Browning's dealt pre-eminently with what may be called his own subject, the experiences of love.

And this quality of Browning's optimism, the quality of detail, is also a very typical quality. Browning's optimism is of that ultimate and unshakeable order that is founded upon the absolute sight, and sound, and smell, and handling of things. If a man had gone up to Browning and asked him with all the solemnity of the eccentric, "Do you think life is worth living?" it is interesting to conjecture what his answer might have been. If he had been for the moment under the influence of the orthodox rationalistic deism of the theologian he would have said, "Existence is justified by its manifest design, its manifest adaptation of means to ends," or, in other words, "Existence is justified by its completeness." If, on the other hand, he had been influenced by his own serious intellectual theories he would have said, "Existence is justified by its air of growth and doubtfulness," or, in other words, "Existence is justified by its incompleteness." But if he had not been influenced in his answer either by the accepted opinions, or by his own opinions, but had simply answered the question "Is life worth living?" with the real, vital answer that awaited it in his own soul, he would have said as likely as not, "Crimson toadstools in Hampshire." Some plain, glowing picture of this sort left on his mind would be his real verdict on what the universe had meant to him. To his traditions hope was traced to order, to his speculations hope was traced to disorder. But to Browning himself hope was traced to something like red toadstools. His mysticism was not of that idle and wordy type which believes that a flower is symbolical of life; it was rather of that deep and eternal type which believes that life, a mere abstraction, is symbolical of a flower. With him the great concrete experiences which God made always come first; his own deductions and speculations about them always second. And in this point we find the real peculiar inspiration of his very original poems.

One of the very few critics who seem to have got near to the actual secret of Browning's optimism is Mr. Santayana in his most interesting book *Interpretations of Poetry and Religion*. He, in contradistinction to the vast mass of Browning's admirers, had discovered what was the real root virtue of Browning's poetry; and the curious thing is, that having discovered that root virtue, he thinks it is a vice. He describes the poetry of Browning most truly as the poetry of barbarism, by which he means the poetry which utters the primeval and indivisible emotions. "For the barbarian is the man who regards his passions as their own excuse for being, who does not domesticate them either by understanding their cause, or by conceiving their ideal goal." Whether this be or be not a good definition of the barbarian, it is an excellent and perfect definition of the poet. It might, perhaps, be suggested that barbarians, as a matter of fact, are generally highly traditional and respectable persons who would not put a feather wrong in their head-gear, and who generally have very few feelings and think very little about those they have. It is when we have grown to a greater and more civilised stature that we begin to realise and put to ourselves intellectually the great feelings that sleep in the depths of us. Thus it is that the literature of our day has steadily advanced towards a passionate simplicity, and we become more primeval as the world grows older, until Whitman writes huge and chaotic psalms to express the sensations of a schoolboy out fishing, and Macterlinck embodies in symbolic dramas the feelings of a child in the dark.

Thus, Mr. Santayana is, perhaps, the most valuable of all the Browning critics. He has gone out of his way to endeavour to realise what it is that repels him in Browning, and he has discovered the fault which none of Browning's opponents have discovered. And in this he has discovered the merit which none of Browning's admirers have discovered. Whether the quality be a good or a bad quality, Mr. Santayana is perfectly right. The whole of Browning's poetry does rest upon primitive feeling; and the only comment to be added is that so does the whole of every one else's poetry. Poetry deals entirely with those great eternal and mainly forgotten wishes which are the ultimate despots of existence. Poetry presents things as they are to our emotions, not as they are to any theory, however plausible, or any argument, however conclusive. If love is in truth a glorious vision, poetry will say that it is a glorious vision, and no philosophers will persuade poetry to say that it is the exaggeration of the instinct of sex. If bereavement is a bitter and continually aching thing, poetry will say that it is so, and no philosophers will persuade poetry to say that it is an evolutionary stage of great biological value. And here comes in the whole value and object of poetry, that it is perpetually challenging all systems with the test of a terrible sincerity. The practical value of poetry is that it is realistic upon a point upon which nothing else can be realistic, the point of the actual desires of man. Ethics is the science of actions, but poetry is the science of motives. Some actions are ugly, and therefore some parts of ethics are ugly. But all motives are beautiful, or present themselves for the moment as beautiful, and therefore all poetry is beautiful. If poetry deals with the basest matter, with the shedding of blood for gold, it ought to suggest the gold as well as the blood. Only poetry can realise motives, because motives are all pictures of happiness. And the supreme and most practical value of poetry is this, that in poetry, as in music, a note is struck which expresses beyond the power of rational statement a condition of mind, and all actions arise from a condition of mind. Prose can only use a large and clumsy notation; it can only say that a man is miserable, or that a man is happy; it is forced to ignore that there are a million diverse kinds of misery and a million diverse kinds of happiness. Poetry alone, with the first throb of its metre, can tell us whether the depression is the kind of depression that drives a man to suicide, or the kind of depression that drives him to the Tivoli. Poetry can tell us whether the happiness is the happiness that sends a man to a restaurant, or the much richer and fuller happiness that sends him to church.

Now the supreme value of Browning as an optimist lies in this that we have been examining, that beyond all his conclusions, and deeper than all his arguments, he was passionately interested in and in love with existence. If the heavens had fallen, and all the waters of the earth run with blood, he would still have been interested in existence, if possible a little more so. He is a great poet of human joy for precisely the reason of which Mr. Santayana complains: that his happiness is primal, and beyond the reach of philosophy. He is something far more convincing, far more comforting, far more religiously significant than an optimist: he is a happy man.

This happiness he finds, as every man must find happiness, in his own way. He does not find the great part of his joy in those matters in which most poets find felicity. He finds much of it in those matters in which most poets find ugliness and vulgarity. He is to a considerable extent the poet of towns. "Do you care for nature much?" a friend of his asked him. "Yes, a great deal," he said, "but for human beings a great deal more." Nature, with its splendid and soothing sanity, has the power of convincing most poets of the essential worthiness of things. There are few poets who, if they escaped from the rowdiest waggonette of trippers, could not be quieted again and exalted by dropping into a small wayside field. The speciality of Browning is rather that he would have been quieted and exalted by the waggonette.

To Browning, probably the beginning and end of all optimism was to be found in the faces in the street. To him they were all the masks of a deity, the heads of a hundred-headed Indian god of nature. Each one of them looked towards some quarter of the heavens, not looked upon by any other eyes. Each one of them wore some expression, some blend of eternal joy and eternal sorrow, not to be found in any other countenance. The sense of the absolute sanctity of human difference was the deepest of all his senses. He was hungrily interested in all human things, but it would have been quite impossible to have said of him that he loved humanity. He did not love humanity but men. His sense of the difference between one man and another would have made the thought of melting them into a lump called humanity simply loathsome and prosaic. It would have been to him like playing four hundred beautiful airs at once. The mixture would not combine all, it would lose all. Browning believed that to every man that ever lived upon this earth had been given a definite and peculiar confidence of God. Each one of us was engaged on secret service; each one of us had a peculiar message; each one of us was the founder of a religion. Of that religion our thoughts, our faces, our bodies, our hats, our boots, our tastes, our virtues, and even our vices, were more or less fragmentary and inadequate expressions.

In the delightful memoirs of that very remarkable man Sir Charles Gavan Duffy, there is an extremely significant and interesting anecdote about Browning, the point of which appears to have attracted very little attention. Duffy was dining with Browning and John Forster, and happened to make some chance allusion to his own adherence to the Roman Catholic faith, when Forster remarked, half jestingly, that he did not suppose that Browning would like him any the better for that. Browning would seem to have opened his eyes with some astonishment. He immediately asked why

Forster should suppose him hostile to the Roman Church. Forster and Duffy replied almost simultaneously, by referring to "Bishop Blougram's Apology," which had just appeared, and asking whether the portrait of the sophistical and self-indulgent priest had not been intended for a satire on Cardinal Wiseman. "Certainly," replied Browning cheerfully, "I intended it for Cardinal Wiseman, but I don't consider it a satire, there is nothing hostile about it." This is the real truth which lies at the heart of what may be called the great sophistical monologues which Browning wrote in later years. They are not satires or attacks upon their subjects, they are not even harsh and unfeeling exposures of them. They are defences; they say or are intended to say the best that can be said for the persons with whom they deal. But very few people in this world would care to listen to the real defence of their own characters. The real defence, the defence which belongs to the Day of Judgment, would make such damaging admissions, would clear away so many artificial virtues, would tell such tragedies of weakness and failure, that a man would sooner be misunderstood and censured by the world than exposed to that awful and merciless eulogy. One of the most practically difficult matters which arise from the code of manners and the conventions of life, is that we cannot properly justify a human being, because that justification would involve the admission of things which may not conventionally be admitted. We might explain and make human and respectable, for example, the conduct of some old fighting politician, who, for the good of his party and his country, acceded to measures of which he disapproved; but we cannot, because we are not allowed to admit that he ever acceded to measures of which he disapproved. We might touch the life of many dissolute public men with pathos, and a kind of defeated courage, by telling the truth about the history of their sins. But we should throw the world into an uproar if we hinted that they had any. Thus the decencies of civilisation do not merely make it impossible to revile a man, they make it impossible to praise him.

Browning, in such poems as "Bishop Blougram's Apology," breaks this first mask of goodness in order to break the second mask of evil, and gets to the real goodness at last; he dethrones a saint in order to humanise a scoundrel. This is one typical side of the real optimism of Browning. And there is indeed little danger that such optimism will become weak and sentimental and popular, the refuge of every idler, the excuse of every ne'er-do-weel. There is little danger that men will desire to excuse their souls before God by presenting themselves before men as such snobs as Bishop Blougram, or such dastards as Sludge the Medium. There is no pessimism, however stern, that is so stern as this optimism, it is as merciless as the mercy of God.

It is true that in this, as in almost everything else connected with Browning's character, the matter cannot be altogether exhausted by such a generalisation as the above. Browning's was a simple character, and therefore very difficult to understand, since it was impulsive, unconscious, and kept no reckoning of its moods. Probably in a great many cases, the original impulse which led Browning to plan a soliloquy was a kind of anger mixed with curiosity; possibly the first charcoal sketch of Blougram was a caricature of a priest. Browning, as we have said, had prejudices, and had a capacity for anger, and two of his angriest prejudices were against a certain kind of worldly clericalism, and against almost every kind of spiritualism. But as he worked upon the portraits at least, a new spirit began to possess him, and he enjoyed every spirited and just defence the men could make of themselves, like triumphant blows in a battle, and towards the end would come the full revelation, and Browning would stand up in the man's skin and testify to the man's ideals. However this may be, it is worth while to notice one very curious error that has arisen in connection with one of the most famous of these monologues.

When Robert Browning was engaged in that somewhat obscure quarrel with the spiritualist Home, it is generally and correctly stated that he gained a great number of the impressions which he afterwards embodied in "Mr. Sludge the Medium." The statement so often made, particularly in the spiritualist accounts of the matter, that Browning himself is the original of the interlocutor and exposer of Sludge, is of course merely an example of that reckless reading from which no one has suffered more than Browning despite his students and societies. The man to whom Sludge addresses his confession is a Mr. Hiram H. Horsefall, an American, a patron of spiritualists, and, as it is more than once suggested, something of a fool. Nor is there the smallest reason to suppose that Sludge considered as an individual bears any particular resemblance to Home considered as an individual. But without doubt "Mr. Sludge the Medium" is a general statement of the view of spiritualism at which Browning had arrived from his acquaintance with Home and Home's circle. And about that view of spiritualism there is something rather peculiar to notice. The poem, appearing as it did at the time when the intellectual public had just become conscious of the existence of spiritualism, attracted a great deal of attention, and aroused a great deal of controversy. The spiritualists called down thunder upon the head of the poet, whom they depicted as a vulgar and ribald lampooner who had not only committed the profanity of sneering at the mysteries of a higher state of life, but the more unpardonable profanity of sneering at the convictions of his own wife. The sceptics, on the other hand, hailed the poem with delight as a blasting exposure of spiritualism, and congratulated the poet on making himself the champion of the sane and scientific view of magic. Which of these two parties was right about the question of attacking the reality of spiritualism it is neither easy nor necessary to discuss. For the simple truth, which neither of the two parties and none of the students of Browning seem to have noticed, is that "Mr. Sludge the Medium" is not an attack upon spiritualism. It would be a great deal nearer the truth, though not entirely the truth, to call it a justification of spiritualism. The whole essence of Browning's method is involved in this matter, and the whole essence of Browning's method is so vitally misunderstood that to say that "Mr. Sludge the Medium" is something like a defence of spiritualism will bear on the face of it the appearance of the most empty and perverse of paradoxes. But so, when we have comprehended Browning's spirit, the fact will be found to be.

The general idea is that Browning must have intended "Sludge" for an attack on spiritual phenomena, because the medium in that poem is made a vulgar and contemptible mountebank, because his cheats are quite openly confessed, and he himself put into every ignominious situation, detected, exposed, throttled, and forgiven. To regard this deduction as sound is to misunderstand Browning at the very start of every poem that he ever wrote. There is nothing that the man loved more, nothing that deserves more emphatically to be called a speciality of Browning, than the utterance of large and noble truths by the lips of mean and grotesque human beings. In his poetry praise and wisdom were perfected not only out of the mouths of babes and sucklings, but out of the mouths of swindlers and snobs. Now what, as a matter of fact, is the outline and development of the poem of "Sludge"? The climax of the poem, considered as a work of art, is so fine that it is quite extraordinary that any one should have missed the point of it, since it is the whole point of the monologue. Sludge the Medium has been caught out in a piece of unquestionable trickery, a piece of trickery for which there is no conceivable explanation or palliation which will leave his moral character intact. He is therefore seized with a sudden resolution, partly angry, partly frightened, and partly humorous, to become absolutely frank, and to tell the whole truth about himself for the first time not only to his dupe, but to himself. He excuses himself for the earlier stages of the trickster's life by a survey of the border-land between truth and fiction, not by any means a piece of sophistry or cynicism, but a perfectly fair statement of an ethical difficulty which does exist. There are some people who think that it must be immoral to admit that there are any doubtful cases of morality, as if a man should refrain from discussing the precise boundary at the upper end of the Isthmus of Panama, for fear the inquiry should shake his belief in the existence of North America. People of this kind quite consistently think Sludge to be merely a scoundrel talking nonsense. It may be remembered that they thought the same thing of Newman. It is actually supposed, apparently in the current use of words, that casuistry is the name of a crime; it does not appear to occur to people that casuistry is a science, and about as much a crime as botany. This tendency to casuistry in Browning's monologues has done much towards establishing for him that reputation for pure intellectualism which has done him so much harm. But casuistry in this sense is not a cold and analytical thing, but a very warm and sympathetic thing. To know what combinations of excuse might justify a man in manslaughter or bigamy, is not to have a callous indifference to virtue; it is rather to have so ardent an admiration for virtue as to seek it in the remotest desert and the darkest incognito.

This is emphatically the case with the question of truth and falsehood raised in "Sludge the Medium." To say that it is sometimes difficult to tell at what point the romancer turns into the liar is not to state a cynicism, but a perfectly honest piece of human observation. To think that such a view involves the negation of honesty is like thinking that red is green, because the two fade into each other in the colours of the rainbow. It is really difficult to decide when we come to the extreme edge of veracity, when and when not it is permissible to create an illusion. A standing example, for instance, is the case of the fairy-tales. We think a father entirely pure and benevolent when he tells his children that a beanstalk grew up into heaven, and a pumpkin turned into a coach. We should consider that he lapsed from purity and benevolence if he told his children that in walking home that evening he had seen a beanstalk grow half-way up the church, or a pumpkin grow as large as a wheelbarrow. Again, few people would object to that general privilege whereby it is permitted to a person in narrating even a true anecdote to work up the climax by any exaggerative touches which really tend to bring it out. The reason of this is that the telling of the anecdote has become, like the telling of the fairy-tale, almost a distinct artistic creation; to offer to tell a story is in ordinary society like offering to recite or play the violin. No one denies that a fixed and genuine moral rule could be drawn up for these cases, but no one surely need be ashamed to admit that such a rule is not entirely easy to draw up. And when a man like Sludge traces much of his moral downfall to the indistinctness of the boundary and the possibility of beginning with a natural extravagance and ending with a gross abuse, it certainly is not possible to deny his right to be heard.

We must recur, however, to the question of the main development of the Sludge self-analysis. He begins, as we have said, by urging a general excuse by the fact that in the heat of social life, in the course of telling tales in the intoxicating presence of sympathisers and believers, he has slid into falsehood almost before he is aware of it. So far as this goes, there is truth in his plea. Sludge might indeed find himself unexpectedly justified if we had only an exact record of how true were the tales told about Conservatives in an exclusive circle of Radicals, or the stories told about Radicals in a circle of indignant Conservatives. But after this general excuse, Sludge goes on to a perfectly cheerful and unfeeling admission of fraud: this principal feeling towards his victims is by his own confession a certain unfathomable contempt for people who are so easily taken in. He professes to know how to lay the foundations for every species of personal acquaintanceship, and how to remedy the slight and trivial slips of making Homer write Greek in noughts and crosses.

> "As, Sir, we somewhat fear he was apt to say
> Before I found the useful book that knows."

It would be difficult to imagine any figure more indecently confessional, more entirely devoid of not only any of the restraints of conscience, but of any of the restraints even of a wholesome personal conceit, than Sludge the Medium. He confesses not only fraud, but things which are to the natural man more difficult to confess even than fraud—effeminacy, futility, physical cowardice. And then, when the last of his loathsome secrets has been told, when he has nothing left either to gain or to conceal, then he rises up into a perfect bankrupt sublimity and makes the great avowal which is the whole pivot and meaning of the poem.

He says in effect: "Now that my interest in deceit is utterly gone, now that I have admitted, to my own final infamy, the frauds that I have practised, now that I stand before you in a patent and open villainy which has something of the disinterestedness and independence of the innocent, now I tell you with the full and impartial authority of a lost soul that I believe that there is something in spiritualism. In the course of a thousand conspiracies, by the labour of a thousand lies, I have discovered that there is really something in this matter that neither I nor any other man understands. I am a thief, an adventurer, a deceiver of mankind, but I am not a disbeliever in spiritualism. I have seen too much for that." This is the confession of faith of Mr. Sludge the Medium. It would be difficult to imagine a confession of faith framed and presented in a more impressive manner. Sludge is a witness to his faith as the old martyrs were witnesses to their faith, but even more impressively. They testified to their religion even after they had lost their liberty, and their eyesight, and their right hands. Sludge testifies to his religion even after he has lost his dignity and his honour.

It may be repeated that it is truly extraordinary that any one should have failed to notice that this avowal on behalf of spiritualism is the pivot of the poem. The avowal itself is not only expressed clearly, but prepared and delivered with admirable rhetorical force:—

"Now for it, then! Will you believe me, though?
You've heard what I confess: I don't unsay
A single word: I cheated when I could,
Rapped with my toe-joints, set sham hands at work,
Wrote down names weak in sympathetic ink.

> Rubbed odic lights with ends of phosphor-match,
> And all the rest ; believe that : believe this,
> By the same token, though it seem to set
> The crooked straight again, unsay the said,
> Stick up what I've knocked down ; I can't help that,
> It's truth ! I somehow vomit truth to-day.
> This trade of mine—I don't know, can't be sure
> But there was something in it, tricks and all ! "

It is strange to call a poem with so clear and fine a climax an attack on spiritualism. To miss that climax is like missing the last sentence in a good anecdote, or putting the last act of *Othello* into the middle of the play. Either the whole poem of "Sludge the Medium" means nothing at all, and is only a lampoon upon a cad, of which the matter is almost as contemptible as the subject, or it means this—that some real experiences of the unseen lie even at the heart of hypocrisy, and that even the spiritualist is at root spiritual.

One curious theory which is common to most Browning critics is that Sludge must be intended for a pure and conscious impostor, because after his confession, and on the personal withdrawal of Mr. Horsefall, he bursts out into horrible curses against that gentleman and cynical boasts of his future triumphs in a similar line of business. Surely this is to have a very feeble notion either of nature or art. A man driven absolutely into a corner might humiliate himself, and gain a certain sensation almost of luxury in that humiliation, in pouring out all his imprisoned thoughts and obscure victories. For let it never be forgotten that a hypocrite is a very unhappy man; he is a man who has devoted himself to a most delicate and arduous intellectual art in which he may achieve masterpieces which he must keep secret, fight thrilling

battles, and win hair's-breadth victories for which he
cannot have a whisper of praise. A really accomplished
impostor is the most wretched of geniuses; he is a
Napoleon on a desert island. A man might surely,
therefore, when he was certain that his credit was
gone, take a certain pleasure in revealing the tricks
of his unique trade, and gaining not indeed credit, but
at least a kind of glory. And in the course of this
self-revelation he would come at last upon that part
of himself which exists in every man—that part which
does believe in, and value, and worship something.
This he would fling in his hearer's face with even
greater pride, and take a delight in giving a kind of
testimony to his religion which no man had ever given
before—the testimony of a martyr who could not hope
to be a saint. But surely all this sudden tempest of
candour in the man would not mean that he would
burst into tears and become an exemplary ratepayer,
like a villain in the worst parts of Dickens. The
moment the danger was withdrawn, the sense of
having given himself away, of having betrayed the
secret of his infamous freemasonry, would add an
indescribable violence and foulness to his reaction of
rage. A man in such a case would do exactly as
Sludge does. He would declare his own shame, declare the truth of his creed, and then, when he realised
what he had done, say something like this:—

"R-r-r, you brute-beast and blackguard! Cowardly scamp!
I only wish I dared burn down the house
And spoil your sniggering!"

and so on, and so on.

He would react like this; it is one of the most
artistic strokes in Browning. But it does not prove
that he was a hypocrite about spiritualism, or that he

was speaking more truthfully in the second outburst than in the first. Whence came this extraordinary theory that a man is always speaking most truly when he is speaking most coarsely? The truth about oneself is a very difficult thing to express, and coarse speaking will seldom do it.

When we have grasped this point about "Sludge the Medium," we have grasped the key to the whole series of Browning's casuistical monologues—*Bishop Blougram's Apology*, *Prince Hohenstiel-Schwangau*, *Fra Lippo Lippi*, *Fifine at the Fair*, *Aristophanes' Apology*, and several of the monologues in *The Ring and the Book*. They are all, without exception, dominated by this one conception of a certain reality tangled almost inextricably with unrealities in a man's mind, and the peculiar fascination which resides in the thought that the greatest lies about a man, and the greatest truths about him, may be found side by side in the same eloquent and sustained utterance.

"For Blougram, he believed, say, half he spoke."

Or, to put the matter in another way, the general idea of these poems is, that a man cannot help telling some truth even when he sets out to tell lies. If a man comes to tell us that he has discovered perpetual motion, or been swallowed by the sea-serpent, there will yet be some point in the story where he will tell us about himself almost all that we require to know.

If any one wishes to test the truth, or to see the best examples of this general idea in Browning's monologues, he may be recommended to notice one peculiarity of these poems which is rather striking. As a whole, these apologies are written in a particularly burly and even brutal English. Browning's love of what is called the ugly is nowhere else so fully and extravagantly indulged. This, like a great many other things for which Browning as an artist is blamed, is perfectly appropriate to the theme. A vain, ill-mannered, and untrustworthy egotist, defending his own sordid doings with his own cheap and weather-beaten philosophy, is very likely to express himself best in a language flexible and pungent, but indelicate and without dignity. But the peculiarity of these loose and almost slangy soliloquies is that every now and then in them there occur bursts of pure poetry which are like a burst of birds singing. Browning does not hesitate to put some of the most perfect lines that he or any-one else have ever written in the English language into the mouths of such slaves as Sludge and Guido Franceschini. Take, for the sake of example, "Bishop Blougram's Apology." The poem is one of the most grotesque in the poet's works. It is intentionally redolent of the solemn materialism and patrician grossness of a grand dinner-party *à deux*. It has many touches of an almost wild bathos, such as the young man who bears the impossible name of Gigadibs. The Bishop, in pursuing his worldly argument for conformity, points out with truth that a condition of doubt is a condition that cuts both ways, and that if we cannot be sure of the religious theory of life, neither can we be sure of the material theory of life, and that in turn is capable of becoming an un-certainty continually shaken by a tormenting sugges-tion. We cannot establish ourselves on rationalism, and make it bear fruit to us. Faith itself is capable of becoming the darkest and most revolutionary of doubts. Then comes the passage:—

> "Just when we are safest, there's a sunset-touch,
> A fancy from a flower-bell, some one's death,
> A chorus ending from Euripides,—
> And that's enough for fifty hopes and fears
> As old and new at once as Nature's self,
> To rap and knock and enter in our soul,
> Take hands and dance there, a fantastic ring,
> Round the ancient idol, on his base again,—
> The grand Perhaps!"

Nobler diction and a nobler meaning could not have been put into the mouth of Pompilia, or Rabbi Ben Ezra. It is in reality put into the mouth of a vulgar, fashionable priest, justifying his own cowardice over the comfortable wine and the cigars.

Along with this tendency to poetry among Browning's knaves, must be reckoned another characteristic, their uniform tendency to theism. These loose and mean characters speak of many things feverishly and vaguely; of one thing they always speak with confidence and composure, their relation to God. It may seem strange at first sight that those who have outlived the indulgence, and not only of every law, but of every reasonable anarchy, should still rely so simply upon the indulgence of divine perfection. Thus Sludge is certain that his life of lies and conjuring tricks has been conducted in a deep and subtle obedience to the message really conveyed by the conditions created by God. Thus Bishop Blougram is certain that his life of panic-stricken and tottering compromise has been really justified as the only method that could unite him with God. Thus Prince Hohenstiel-Schwangau is certain that every dodge in his thin string of political dodges has been the true means of realising what he believes to be the will of God. Every one of these meagre swindlers, while admitting a failure in all things relative, claims an awful alliance with the Absolute. To many it will at first sight appear a dangerous doctrine indeed. But, in truth, it is a most solid and noble and salutary doctrine, far less dangerous than its opposite. Every one on this earth should believe, amid whatever madness or moral failure, that his life and temperament have some object on the earth. Every one on the earth should believe that he has something to give to the world which cannot otherwise be given. Every one should, for the good of men and the saving of his own soul, believe that it is possible, even if we are the enemies of the human race, to be the friends of God. The evil wrought by this mystical pride, great as it often is, is like a straw to the evil wrought by a materialistic self-abandonment. The crimes of the devil who thinks himself of immeasurable value are as nothing to the crimes of the devil who thinks himself of no value. With Browning's knaves we have always this eternal interest, that they are real somewhere, and may at any moment begin to speak poetry. We are talking to a peevish and garrulous sneak; we are watching the play of his paltry features, his evasive eyes, and babbling lips. And suddenly the face begins to change and harden, the eyes glare like the eyes of a mask, the whole face of clay becomes a common mouthpiece, and the voice that comes forth is the voice of God, uttering His everlasting soliloquy.

INDEX

A

Agamemnon of Æschylus, The, 120.
Alliance, The Holy, 89.
"Andrea del Sarto," 83.
Aristophanes' Apology, 120, 199.
Arnold, Matthew, 41, 55, 56.
Asolando, 132.
Asolo (Italy), 42, 131.
"At the Mermaid," 117.
Austria, 88, 89.

B

"Bad Dreams," 138.
Balaustion's Adventure, 119-120.
Barrett, Arabella, 74, 119.
Barrett, Edward Moulton, 58 *seq.*, 70, 73, 74, 76, 79.
Beardsley, Mr. Aubrey, 149.
Bells and Pomegranates, 105.
"Ben Ezra," 23, 201.
Birrell, Mr. Augustine, 160.
"Bishop Blougram," 51, 189.
Bishop Blougram's Apology, 188, 189, 199, 200.
Blot on the 'Scutcheon, A, 53.
Boyd, Mr., 62.
Browning, Robert: birth and family history, 3; theories as to his descent, 4-8; a typical Englishman of the middle class, 9; his immediate ancestors, 10 *seq.*; education, 12; boyhood and youth, 17; first poems, *Incondita,* 17; romantic spirit, 18; publication of *Pauline,* 20; friendship with literary men, 21; *Paracelsus,* 22; introduction to literary world, 25; his earliest admirers, 26; friendship with Carlyle, 26; *Strafford,* 27; *Sordello,* 34; *Pippa Passes,* 43; *Dramatic Lyrics,* 45; *The Return of the Druses,* 51; *A Blot on the 'Scutcheon,* 53; correspondence with Elizabeth Barrett, 62 *seq.*; their first meeting, 70; marriage and elopement, 78, 79; life in Italy, 81 *seq.*; love of Italy, 82, 85 *seq.*; sympathy with Italian Revolution, 90; attitude towards spiritualism, 91 *seq.*, 113, 190-199; death of his wife, 103; returns to England, 105; *The Ring and the Book,* 110; culmination of his literary fame, 110, 117; life in society, 110; elected Fellow of Balliol, 117; honoured by the great Universities, 118; *Balaustion's Adventure,* 119-120; *Aristophanes' Apology,* 120; *The Agamemnon of Æschylus,* 120; *Prince Hohenstiel - Schwangau,* 121; *Red - Cotton Night - Cap Country,* 122; *Fifine at the Fair,* 124; *The Inn Album,* 125; *Pacchiarotto, and How He Worked in Distemper,* 125; *La Saisiaz,* 127; *The Two Poets of Croisic,* 127; *Dramatic Idylls,*

127; *Jocoseria*, 127; *Ferishtah's Fancies*, 127; *Parleyings with Certain People of Importance in their Day*, 128; accepts post of Foreign Correspondent to the Royal Academy, 129; goes to Llangollen with his sister, 130; last journey to Italy, 130; death at Venice, 132; publication of *Asolando*, 132; his conversation, 36; vanity, 33, 36; faults and virtues, 40, 55; his interest in Art, 82 *seq.*; his varied accomplishments, 84-85; personality and presence, 18, 33, 112 *seq.*; his prejudices, 113-116; his occasional coarseness, 116; politics, 86 *seq.*; Browning as a father, 105; as dramatist, 52; as a literary artist, 133 *seq.*; his use of the grotesque, 48, 140, 143, 148 *seq.*; his failures, 141; artistic originality, 136, 143, 158; keen sense of melody and rhythm, 145 *seq.*; ingenuity in rhyming, 152; his buffoonery, 154; obscurity, 154 *seq.*; his conception of the Universe, 175; philosophy, 177 *seq.*; optimism, 179 *seq.*; his love poetry, 49; his knaves, 51, 201-202; the key to his casuistical monologues, 199.

Browning, Life of (Mrs. Orr), 92.

Browning, Robert (father of the poet), 10, 119.

Browning, Mrs., *née* Wiedermann (mother), 11, 82.

Browning, Anna (sister), 14, 105.

Browning, Elizabeth Barrett (wife), 57 *seq.*, 91-99, 101, 103, 116, 119, 129, 131.

Browning Society, 129.

Burns, Robert, 169-170.

Byron, 11, 38, 141, 143.

Byronism, 19, 117.

C

"Caliban," 9, 120.
"Caliban upon Setebos," 93, **135**, 138.
Camberwell, 3, 8, 19.
"Caponsacchi," 108.
Carlyle, Thomas, 12, 16, 17, 26, 55, 56, 87, 115.
Carlyle, Mrs., 26.
"Cavalier Tunes," 46.
Cavour, 86, 90, 103.
Charles I., 28, 29.
Chaucer, 117.
"Childe Roland to the Dark Tower came," 159.
Christmas Eve, 105.
Church in Italy, The, 88.
"Clive," 127.
Clough, Arthur Hugh, 56.
Colombe's Birthday, 32.
Corelli, Miss Marie, 38.
Cromwell, Oliver, 73.

D

Darwin, 23, 39.
Dickens, 16.
"Djabal," 51, 52.
Domett, Alfred, 21.
"Dominus Hyacinthus de Archangelis," 161.
Dramatic Idylls, 127.
Dramatic Lyrics, 45-50.
Dramatis Personæ, 105.
Duffy, Sir Charles Gavan, 187, 188.

E

Edinburgh Review, 122.
"Englishman in Italy, The," 150.

F

"Fears and Scruples," 126, 138.
"Ferishtah's Fancies," 138.
Fifine at the Fair, 9, 13, 51, 124, 199.
Fitzgerald, Edward, 116, 131.

INDEX

Flight of the Duchess, The, 18.
Florence, 81, 94.
Forster, John, 26.
Foster, John, 187, 188.
Fox, Mr. Johnson, 20.
Fox, Mrs. Bridell, 33.
"Fra Lippo," 51.
Fra Lippo Lippi, 83, 199.
French Revolution, 87.
Furnivall, Dr., 7, 129.

G

"Garden Fancies," 46.
Garibaldi, 86, 89.
Gilbert, W. S., 144.
Gissing, Mr. George, 165.
Gladstone, 117.
Golden Treasury (Palgrave), 168.
Goldsmith, 169, 170.
Gordon, General, 90.
"Guido Franceschini," 106, 120, 200.

H

Henley, Mr., 148.
"Heretic's Tragedy, The," 137.
Hickey, Miss E. H., 129.
"Holy Cross Day," 153.
Home, Daniel (spiritualist), 93-97, 113, 190, 191.
Home, Daniel, *Incidents of my Life*, [93 *seq*.
Horne, 26.
Houghton, Lord, 129.
"House," 138.
"Householder, The," 138.
"How they brought the good News from Ghent to Aix," 46.
Hudibras (Butler), 57.
Hugo, Victor, 17.
Hunt, Leigh, 26.

I

Incondita, 17.
Inn Album, The, 125.
Instans Tyrannus, 9.

Italy, 85 *seq*.
Italian Revolution, 88 *seq*.
"Iván Ivánovitch," 127.

J

Jameson, Mrs., 75.
Jerrold, Douglas, 34.
Jocoseria, 127.
Jowett, Dr., 118.
Julius Cæsar (Shakespeare), 28.
"Juris Doctor Bottinius," 161.

K

Keats, 15, 16, 19, 137, 142.
Kenyon, Mr., 22, 58, 69-70, 74, 76.
King Victor and King Charles, 32.
Kipling, Rudyard, 142.
Kirkup, Seymour, 103.

L

L'Aiglon, 28.
"Laboratory, The," 47, 143.
Landor, 26, 56, 93, 101-103.
La Saisiaz, 127.
Letters, The Browning, 63.
Liberalism, 86.
"Lines to Edward Fitzgerald," 131.
Llangollen, 130.
Lockhart, 112.
"Lost Leader, The," 46.
"Lover's Quarrel, A," 50.
"Luigi," 45.
Lytton, Lord (novelist), 91.

M

Macready, 17, 27, 53.
Maeterlinck, 164, 184.
Manning, Cardinal, 91.
Mary Queen of Scots, 29.
"Master Hugues of Saxe-Gotha," 147.
"May and Death," 21.
Mazzini, 89.
Men and Women, 105.
Meredith, George, 156, 165.

Mill, John Stuart, 26, 56.
Milsand, 119.
Milton, 137.
Monckton-Milnes, 26, 100,
Mr. Sludge the Medium, 82, 96, 120, 190-199.
"Muléykeh," 127.
"My Star," 138.

N

"Nationality in Drinks," 46, 138.
Napoleon, 42, 89.
Napoleon III., 56, 92, 121.
"Never the Time and the Place," 127.
Newman, Cardinal, 193.
Norwood, 18.

O

"Ode on the Intimations of Immortality" (Wordsworth), 136.
"Ode on a Grecian Urn" (Keats), 137.
"Old Masters in Florence," 177.
"One Word More," 65.
Orr, Mrs., 72.

P

Pacchiarotto, and How He Worked in Distemper, 125, 126, 152.
Paracelsus, 22, 25, 26, 41, 47, 158.
"Paracelsus," 24, 25.
Painting, Poems on, 83.
Palgrave, Francis, 117.
Paris, 94.
Parleyings with certain Persons of Importance in their Day, 22, 128, 158.
Pauline, 20, 21, 37, 41, 51.
"Pheidippides," 127.
Phelps (actor), 53.
"Pictor Ignotus," 83.
"Pied Piper of Hamelin, The," 153.
"Pippa," 45, 120.
Pippa Passes, 18, 45, 47, 51, 137.

Pisa, 81.
Pius IX., Church under, 88.
Plato, 21, 23.
Poe, Edgar Allan, 144.
Poetry, Pessimistic school of, 130.
"Pompilia," 201.
Pope, 11, 20, 57.
"Portrait, A," 138.
Prince Hohenstiel-Schwangau, 121, 122.
Princess, The (Tennyson), 148.
"Prometheus Unbound" (Shelley), 137.
Prussia, 88, 89.
Puritans, 30.
Pym, 28, 30.

R

"Rabbi Ben Ezra," 201.
Red-Cotton Night-Cap Country, 122-124.
Return of the Druses, The, 51-53.
Revolution, The French, 15; Italian, 90.
Ring and the Book, The, 85, 106, 109, 123, 137, 160-176.
Ripert-Monclar, Comte de, 22, 93.
Roman Church, 114, 187, 188.
Rossetti, 163.
Royalists, 30.
Ruskin, 16, 55, 56, 91, 115.
Russia, 88.

S

Sand, George, 9, 94.
Santayana's, Mr., *Interpretations of Poetry and Religion*, 183-186.
"Sebald," 45.
Shakespeare, 17, 57.
Shakespeare Society, 129.
Sharp, Mr. William, 133.
Shaw, Mr. Bernard, 165.
Shelley, 15, 16, 17, 19, 56, 136, 141, 143.
"Shop," 138.

"Sibrandus Schafnaburgensis," 138.
Silverthorne (Browning's cousin), 21.
"Sludge," 51, 52, 150, 189, 200.
Smith, Elder (publishers), 110.
"Soliloquy of the Spanish Cloister, The," 47.
"Sonnets from the Portuguese," 65.
Sordello, 23, 34, 42.
Speech, Free, 173.
Spenser, 142.
Spiritualism, 9, 91, 113, 190.
"Statue and the Bust, The," 109.
Sterne, 117.
Stevenson, Robert Louis, 60, 114.
Strafford, 27 seq., 37.
"Strafford," 28, 29, 30.
Swinburne, 56, 116, 142, 143.

T

Tait's Magazine, 20.
Talfourd, Sergeant, 26.
Tennyson, 27, 34, 55, 117, 141, 142, 143, 148.
Thackeray, Miss, 123.
"Through the Metidja to Abd-el-Kadr," 46.
Time's Revenges, 9, 93.
Tolstoi, 115.

Tristram Shandy (Sterne), 163.
Two Poets of Croisic, The, 127.

U

University College, 14.
"Up jumped Tokay" (poem quoted), 140.

V

Venice, 131.
Victor of Sardinia, King, 23.
Vogler, Abt, 23.

W

Water Babies (Kingsley), 8.
Watts, Mr. G. F., 112.
Whitman, Walt, 21, 43, 49, 114, 165, 184.
"Why I am a Liberal" (sonnet), 86.
Wiedermann, William, 12.
Wiseman, Cardinal, 188.
Wimbledon Common, 18.
Wordsworth, 69, 136, 141, 143.
Wordsworth Society, 129.

Y

"Youth and Art," 50, 109.

Z

Zola, 164.